At a time when the Christian family is under attack from every angle, Timothy Paul Jones has issued a clarion call for churches to partner with parents to develop a Christ-centered worldview in their children's lives—but he doesn't stop there. He also provides the tools that church leaders will need to implement this vision in their day-by-day practices of ministry, beginning in their own homes. Theologically grounded yet deeply practical, *Family Ministry Field Guide* is a much-needed book.

—James Garlow, Ph.D., senior pastor, Skyline Wesleyan Church

Family Ministry Field Guide is a practical tool for church leaders to question how they equip families to disciple their children. The information is not reactionary, relying on the latest trends or statistics, but instead built upon how the gospel can impact families in a real way.

—Jeff Hutchings, director of family ministry, The Journey, Tower Grove campus

Built on careful study of God's Word and practical wisdom from personal life, *Family Ministry Field Guide* will educate, equip, and inspire church leaders and whole congregations to honor Jesus through effective family ministry. By centering family ministry on the gospel of Jesus Christ, Timothy Paul Jones avoids the trap of idolizing family that comes at the expense of effective mission. This book is not about replacing program-centered ministry with family-centered ministry. Instead we are called to a gospel-centered ministry that clarifies the goals of both parents and churches. More than raising healthy citizens or retaining church members, our goal in family ministry is to see children serving alongside their parents and in the fellowship of the church as missional disciples of Jesus for the glory of God. This book doesn't just provide a simple agenda of new programs to employ but urges churches to pursue a change of culture. We're reminded that real culture change takes time. Yet we're not just left with idealistic dreams but given practical steps to pursue, complete with discussion outlines to work through together as a congregation. This book has given me many helpful ideas to implement. More significantly though, through drawing us to Scripture, it has painted the vision of God's plan for children, families, and congregations that summons my faith, drives me to prayer, and inspires me to action. It's a highly recommended guide for both the theory and practice of family ministry.

—Rev. Graham Stanton, principal, Youthworks College

I found in *Family Ministry Field Guide* an excellent resource for pastors of family ministry and a call for the church to partner with families, not just minister to them, in such a way that the whole family . . . reflects Christ in their home. It is an excellent guide for parents, pastors, and professors of family ministry, providing a contemporary approach for the contemporary family.

—Jim Estep, Ph.D., professor of Christian education, Lincoln Christian College and Seminary

What a practical book for pastors and church leaders who want to be intentional about equipping parents to disciple children! The book helps you understand the challenge of today's families and the different models of family ministry. But its real value is the practical exercises and discussion questions that guide a church in developing its own strategy for discipling all generations.

—Daryl Eldridge, Ph.D., president, Rockbridge Seminary

D0388739

Jones' *Family Ministry Field Guide* will help thousands of Generation X parents who are taking back the role of leading their children spiritually. Raising kids to love God and others takes focus and commitment. This book will give parents the information . . . necessary to make the whole experience of family discipleship much simpler and more manageable.

—Shane Garrison, Ed.D., assistant professor of educational ministries,
Campbellsville University School of Theology

Dr. Timothy Paul Jones has a balanced and prophetic voice about what is happening in the average Christian church and home. He cuts through the false motivations and statistical myths that have motivated many in the family ministry movement. What he offers instead is a refreshing gospel-driven perspective on family ministry—one with the goal of equipping families to be outposts of God's mission in the world. His perspective is *Orange* with a theological edge. Dr. Jones' skill as a teacher and a researcher is clear in this book. His practical and relevant counsel is peppered with fresh statistical research. My prayer is that many churches and ministers will be transformed for Christ's sake because of this important work.

—Jared Kennedy, SojournKids pastor, Sojourn Community Church

Timothy Paul Jones' latest offering, *Family Ministry Field Guide,* fills an important niche in the growing field of family ministry. Informed but readable, it threads the needle of providing both professors and practitioners with a resource that is biblically faithful, theologically thoughtful, historically informed, and practically relevant.

Like a workman, Jones deliberately builds a type of historical theology of family ministry by drawing from the titans of Christian history, while interspersing those grand thoughts with common-sense reflections on parenting, shepherding, and formation from contemporary leaders and everyday people. In sum, *Family Ministry Field Guide* becomes a wonderful weaving of biblical principles, with strong social-science research and practical anecdotes.

While valuing intergenerational interaction, it establishes a framework for local church-based family ministry that places a priority on the home as the centerpiece of spiritual formation. It is my opinion that resources like this can help provide solid solutions on how churches and households of faith can engage in ministry to help address what may be the primary crisis of our age: the disintegration of the family.

—Freddy Cardoza, Ph.D., department chair and associate professor of
Christian education, Talbot School of Theology, Biola University

This is simply the best book I have ever read on family ministry. Every pastor and church leader of families should read it, then get it into the hands of every family in the church. In *Family Ministry Field Guide,* Timothy Paul Jones challenges our assumptions about what we think "works" in family ministry, then stirs an appetite for something far greater: a vision to transform our families through the power of the gospel. There is no improving on Dr. Jones' vision: "The goal is Jesus, the center is the gospel, and the family is the means." Yet Jones gives more than a catch phrase in *Family Ministry Field Guide*; he tells you how it's done.

—Marty Machowski, family life pastor, Covenant Fellowship Church, and author of
Long Story Short: Ten-Minute Devotions to Draw Your Family to God

Timothy Paul Jones' *Family Ministry Field Guide* is an appeal to ministers to embrace a model of ministry that engages with individuals and families in partnership with parents who are recognized and resourced as the primary disciplers of their children. It's a guide to help them work out how effective their current practice is.

Jones does not pretend to offer a quick or easy fix. Instead the book methodically works through planning and implementing a God-honoring, Christ-focused, family-equipping ministry, while supplying encouragement and direction to help overcome some of the obstacles and to avoid some of the pitfalls that are likely to come with the sort of paradigm shift that such a change is likely to entail.

Jones asks challenging and provocative but helpful questions that have emerged from his own experiences in ministry and from his research as seminary professor of leadership and church ministry. As the reader takes time to stop, consider, and reflect, the questions become an invitation to reorder and reprioritize ministry so that effort and direction is spent in promoting the growth and development of Christian community rather than in simply trying to preserve the status quo.

This is not just a book for those who recognize the need to reorient and reenvision their ministries. It also offers advice and guidance for those who are already pursuing patterns of ministry that are more closely modelled on the New Testament paradigm than they are on models from educational institutions or the business world. It is a book that will serve well as an entry level textbook for family ministry and one that will continue to stimulate and encourage in the years to come.

—Andy Stirrup, academic registrar, Youthworks College

In *Family Ministry Field Guide*, Timothy Paul Jones gives us a prequel of sorts for churches who are contemplating moving in the direction of family ministry. This book will help churches (and especially leaders) begin from the planning stages, with specific battle plans for ministries, to develop and to equip ministry teams and lay people alike. Jones' family-equipping ministry model will not only make families stronger and more unified, but the churches that implement these ideas will be stronger and more unified as well. The ideas and tools included in the book will equip family ministries that already exist to become more focused in their approaches and strategies. As I consult with churches across the country, I will recommend this book as a beginning point for preparation for the movement toward family ministry, as well as for churches with existing family ministries to become stronger.

—Jack Hardcastle, president, National Association of Family Ministries, and family minister, Hillcrest Church of Christ

"What do we do first?" is what Timothy Paul Jones says is one of the toughest questions he faces from ministry leaders across the country. In writing this book, the answer to that question just got easier. This is a good place to start. I thank God for Dr. Jones and the grace that has been given him for educating and equipping the church and the home as we pursue the joy of the next generation together.

—David Michael, pastor for parenting and family discipleship, Bethlehem Baptist Church

As I read *Family Ministry Field Guide: How Your Church Can Equip Parents to Make Disciples* by Timothy Paul Jones, I found myself seeing the content from several different perspectives. I realized I was reading this helpful book as a professor of family ministry, as a person with experience in church and parachurch ministry, as a certified family life educator, and not least of all as a parent. Timothy's work is edifying from each one of these points of view.

The introduction of the book sets the course by demonstrating the relevance of the content for contemporary family ministry and its eternal significance. This very simple approach gives the reader a sense of the potential lasting value of what is proposed in subsequent chapters of the book. Along the way, Timothy provides insightful questions and helpful, real-world exercises which can orient ministers, educators, and parents toward a family ministry perspective. *Family Ministry Field Guide* presents a very practical process by which churches can begin to implement a viable family ministry, specifically focused on enhancing parenting and the "equipping of Christian households to function as outposts of God's mission in the world."

Timothy reveals his heart for family through his personal, enlightening illustrations and his clear desire to work beyond what appear to be whole and healthy families. His awareness of God's plan sets the foundation for the process toward a family ministry perspective. His recognition that family ministry must flow from who leaders are with their families establishes much needed authenticity. His value for intergenerational experiences provides the context in which family ministry can thrive.

Timothy is very clear that this book does not advocate the introduction of myriad new programs. He is forthright in noting the time, effort, and energy needed to develop what he is suggesting. At the same time, I am encouraged that it is first of all worthwhile and secondly, doable. Whether a person reads this book as a minister, educator, or parent, the content, recommendations, and vision will likely stir the heart and mind to actively integrate family ministry into everyday life.

—Gregory A. Delort, Ph.D., CFLE, professor of family ministry and
associate dean of academics, Manhattan Christian College

FAMILY MINISTRY FIELD GUIDE

HOW YOUR CHURCH CAN EQUIP PARENTS TO MAKE DISCIPLES

Timothy Paul Jones

wesleyan
publishing
house

Indianapolis, Indiana

Copyright © 2011 by Timothy Paul Jones
Published by Wesleyan Publishing House
Indianapolis, Indiana 46250
Printed in the United States of America
ISBN: 978-0-89827-457-8

Library of Congress Cataloging-in-Publication Data

Jones, Timothy P. (Timothy Paul)
  Family ministry field guide : how the church can equip parents to make disciples / Timothy Paul Jones.
      p. cm.
  Includes bibliographical references.
  ISBN 978-0-89827-457-8
1. Church work with families. 2. Christian education of children. 3. Christian education--Home training.
I. Title.
  BV4438.J66 2011
  259'.1--dc22
                              2011002520

This book is published in association with Nappaland Literary Agency, an independent literary agency
dedicated to producing works that are: Authentic, Relevant, Eternal. For more information about Nappaland,
go to http://www.nappaland.com.

To my daughters
Hannah,
the gift for whom I prayed so long;
a living reminder of the grace of God
beyond anything I could have deserved,
and
Skylar,
in our family, so newly a part
yet so quickly entwined in my heart;
so unexpected, yet so welcome.

CONTENTS

Foreword — 11

Introduction: The Gap in Your Church — 15

Foundation 1: Map the Gap — **21**

1. What Families in Your Church Are Doing—and Not Doing—When You're Not Looking — 23

2. What Family Ministry Is and Why It's Worth It — 31

Foundation 2: Rethink Your Goal — **41**

3. Why *Not* to Do Family Ministry — 43

4. How to Find the Right Motivation — 53

Foundation 3: Frame Your Ministry in God's Story Line — **67**

5. Discover Who Your Children Really Are — 69

6. The Split in God's Story Line — 81

Foundation 4: Give Parents the Guidance They Need — **93**

7. We're Supposed to Do That at Home? — 95

8. A Matter of Training and a Matter of Time — 101

9. Providing What Parents Really Need — 109

Foundation 5: Transition to Family-Equipping — **123**

10. Killing the One-Eared Mickey Mouse — 125

11. Family-Equipping Transition 1: Be — 137

12. Family-Equipping Transition 2a: Equip Families for Faith Talks — 151

13. Family-Equipping Transition 2b: Equip Families for Faith Walks and Faith Processes — 161

14. Family-Equipping Transition 3: Acknowledge — 171

15. Family-Equipping Transition 4: Synchronize
   (with W. Ryan Steenburg)   179

Afterword   197

Twelve Tools to Equip Families   199

Worksheet A: Family Discipleship Perceptions and Practices Survey   201

Worksheet B: Motives Matter   204

Worksheet C: Living in God's Story Line   206

Worksheet D: What Message Are We Sending?   208

Worksheet E: TIE Your Ministry Together   210

Acknowledgements   212

Appendix: Survey Methodology and Results   215

Notes   219

About the Author   223

FOREWORD

When my book *Family-Based Youth Ministry* was first published in 1994, my children were thirteen, nine, and five. Most of what came out in that book was theory—theory that I fully believed in, but untested theory nonetheless.

Today, I am a grandfather, and my kids are all adults whom I love, and whom, more importantly, I really like. Each with ministries of their own, I look up to them more each year, so thrilled about the ways they have surpassed my wife and me in the ways they live out their love for God.

But between the "then" and the "now," between the theory and the practice, was not an endless series of victories.

We felt our parenting failures acutely. We knew the alluring temptation to airbrush our failures so that we might look a little less like we are and a little more like galvanized experts who write books about Christian families.

More than anything else, one factor made the difference for our kids. It kept us honest and gave us comfort. It allowed us to accept our brokenness and alerted us to our own excuses. It provided a place to fall apart and be pulled back together again.

That one factor was our church family.

Our church family has frequently heard me say: "I shudder to think where our babies would be today if it hadn't been for you."

My kids grew up in the stew of family-based youth ministry. They grew up surrounded by their imperfect parents in an imperfect church with imperfect programs and imperfect results. It's not that we somehow got the programs or the structure or the model "right." What we did get right was the almost magical alchemy of a church that empowers parents and stands in the gap when they don't happen to feel so powerful.

Sadly, much that passes for "family ministry" today is just a thinly veiled strategy for making parents feel guilty by giving them a long litany of more things they have to do. I've discovered, like you, that most parents don't need another thing to feel guilty about. And most parents of teenagers feel guilty enough already without any help from zealous crusaders for family ministry.

What broken parents like you and me need most is a Christian community that raises the water level of normal so naturally that all our families rise together.

BUT HOW?

Over the last fifteen years or so, there has been one question that I have heard at least ten times more than any other. It usually goes something like this: "Okay, I'm convinced. Partnering with families in youth ministry really does make sense. But how in the world do I actually do it?"

This book is one of the clearest answers to that question I've ever seen.

What I love about what Timothy has done is that he invites our churches into processes for architecting healthy ministries that support and empower families as they seek to disciple their children. But he doesn't just leave us there. He offers ways this approach can actually impact families who might be totally disconnected from the faith.

This book is not about using whatever works to get more kids to show up to our churches. Instead, Timothy has invited us to consider strategies that are theologically grounded, multigenerational, and deeply anchored ways of impacting the next generation with a faith that actually sticks.

The beauty of this resource is precisely the fact that it does not work, at least not in the typical sense of merely attracting more numbers. The beauty, indeed the miracle, of this book is that its principles will work even when its recommendations may not seem to work.

If what you're looking for are blockbuster programs that will guarantee you crowds of families who will embrace every program and every new initiative you try, then what you will read in this guide is not really going to help. But if you are unafraid of the messiness that is always a part of authentic discipleship, if you are myopically committed to seeing young people grow toward mature Christian adults, if you are willing to accept your own need for grace and for partners in parenting and ministry, this book presents you with a plan that will change the way you think about family, church, and ministry forever.

—Mark DeVries

Mark DeVries is the author of Family-Based Youth Ministry, *the founder of Youth Ministry Architects (www.ymarchitects.com), and has served as the youth pastor at First Presbyterian Church in Nashville, Tennessee for the past twenty-five years.*

INTRODUCTION
THE GAP IN YOUR CHURCH

So you're thinking about moving your ministry in a more family friendly direction.

Perhaps you've watched one too many Christian parents disengage from their children's spiritual development and you're looking for some tools to turn this trend around. Perhaps you've seen too many Christian students drop out of church after a few months at a local college or university and you're ready to reverse the drift.

Or maybe you heard the phrase "family ministry" for the first time at a recent conference or retreat and you want to learn more. It could be that you're even a bit skeptical—after all, if your church moves toward family ministry, what does that mean for ministries to youth and children? And what about the young people whose families aren't involved in church at all? Will an emphasis on family ministry exclude them from experiencing your church's fellowship?

Perhaps you're feeling frustrated with the ministry that you've been called to lead. The burning bush of God's call seems to have died down to a few smoldering embers, blown about in the desert sand. You wonder if family ministry might be the spark that reignites your passion.

Whatever your reasons for picking up this book, please pick up a writing utensil too; you'll need it from time to time as you're reading. Let's begin your journey with a simple exercise to spark your thinking: locate the boxes labeled "The Way Things Probably Are" and "The Way Things Ought to Be" at the end of this introduction. In the box that says, "The Way Things Ought to Be," list the devotional practices and deeds of service that ought to characterize a Christ-centered family.

Be specific! Don't simply write "prayer," but list how often, where, and with whom you think family prayer ought to occur. Is it parents with their children? Is it husband and wife with each other? Maybe it's the entire family together? Is it all of the above?

Family devotional times are great, but how many times should you do them each month? Who should lead them? What should these times include?

Once you've listed the habits of highly devoted families in the right-hand box, look at the box titled "The Way Things Probably Are."

For each habit you listed on the right, write in the left-hand box the percentage of parents in your church that you estimate actually practice that habit with their children. Be completely honest.

Then compare your two lists. What do you notice? If your responses are typical, the results may be a bit discouraging. In many churches, there is a significant gap between what is and what ought to be. Scripture clearly calls parents to train their children in the faith and to nurture their children's souls (Deut. 6:4–9; Eph. 6:4). Yet few parents are actively involved in their children's spiritual development. Even fewer can be said to function as primary faith trainers in their children's lives.

Now, in the space between the boxes, write two simple words: "Why?" and "How?" Those are the questions that I have wrestled with for several years now: Why is there such a gap between what should be happening in Christian households and what families in our churches are actually doing? And how can churches partner with parents to close that chasm?

After multiple phases of research, some clear answers to these questions are beginning to emerge. A few findings were worse than I anticipated, some were far better, and a couple came as complete surprises. But in the end, I was encouraged—not because so many families were engaging in spiritual practices at home (they weren't!), but because it became clear that gospel-centered change is possible.

Over the past three years, I have had the privilege of working with many ministries and entire congregations that are effectively equipping parents to actively engage in their children's spiritual development. What you are about to read in this book will show you how real-life churches have narrowed the gap between the biblical ideal and the actual practices.

What we will explore in the first couple of chapters is the precise magnitude of the gap between what is and what ought to be. Two recent research projects have provided a snapshot of what's happening (and not happening) in Christian homes. That research will help us focus on areas where families are falling short of a biblical ideal.

After we explore the size and shape of the gap, we will also consider some additional questions: What should motivate us to change our ministry practices? What does the biblical and theological framework for these changes look like? Why is it that parents aren't actively engaged in their children's spiritual development?

The last chapters of this book will investigate common characteristics and transitional patterns in effective family ministries. What you learn from these characteristics and patterns will provide you with the tools you need to guide your ministry toward equipping the families in your congregation.

Are you ready to begin?

If so, take a seat in my car and come with me!

Our first stop is a coffee shop not too far from my house.

Discipleship: A personal and intentional process in which one or more Christians guide unbelievers or less-mature believers to embrace and apply the gospel in every part of their lives. Discipleship is a process that includes personal profession of faith in Jesus Christ, as he has been revealed to us in Scripture. Discipleship involves developing perspectives and practices that reflect the mind of Christ. The gospel, expressed and applied in the context of the community of faith, is the center point of discipleship; conformity to Jesus Christ is the goal of discipleship; "spiritual development" and "Christian formation" describe progress toward this goal.

SKETCH THE SITUATION

The Way Things Probably Are

SKETCH THE SITUATION

The Way Things Ought to Be

FOUNDATION 1
MAP THE GAP

WHAT FAMILIES IN YOUR CHURCH ARE DOING—AND NOT DOING— WHEN YOU'RE NOT LOOKING

Cosmic combat occurs every Friday morning at a coffee shop a few blocks from my home. If you happen to be ordering your mocha latte during this episode of intergalactic warfare, you might not even notice. Neither arms nor armor can be seen at the epicenter of this celestial struggle. No lightsabers are visible, and no voices are raised. At the nexus of the battle, there is only a man of not-quite-average height in one chair, a bubbly and beautiful middle school girl in another, and a Bible and a couple of ceramic mugs on the table between them.

Do not let such mundane appearances misguide you: This is cosmic combat. When I sit at that table with my daughter, building on a week of family devotions and father-daughter discussions, I am at war. This is not war *with* my daughter; it is war *for* my child's soul.

Even as I train Hannah to take up her cross and root her identity in Jesus Christ, the surrounding culture calls her to celebrate immaturity, smirk at sin, and center her passions on pleasures that will slip away. This is war because the same serpentine dragon in that celestial conflict that John glimpsed on Patmos who longed to consume the fruit of Mary's womb also wants to devour my children (Rev. 12:1–9). His weapons in this conflict are neither the priests of Molech nor the soldiers of Herod (Jer. 32:35–36; Matt. 2:16). The Enemy's weapons in my child's life are slickly promoted celebrities and commercials that subtly but surely corrode her soul. What we wrestle against in this battle is not "flesh and blood, but against the rulers, against the authorities, against the cosmic powers over this dark world, against the spiritual forces of evil in the heavenly places" (Eph. 6:12).

I am able to remove some of these influences from Hannah's life for now, but I cannot and should not shield her from them forever. What I can do is guide her to love what is good, beautiful, and true. I can train her in the fear and reverence of God. I can constantly call her attention to the gospel. And that's precisely what I work to do—not only week-by-week in the café on Dutchman's Lane, but also moment-by-moment in conversations about everything from the latest superhero film to the implications of Daniel's prophecies. These may look like meetings for hazelnut coffee and whole-grain bagels, but what happens here is nothing less than the preparation and execution of a cosmic battle plan. Every week, every day, this is war.

SKETCH THE SITUATION

What intentional practices of family devotions or discipleship have happened in your home in the past week? List each one.

Sunday:

Monday:

Tuesday:

Wednesday:

Thursday:

Friday:

Saturday:

What on your list reflects God's good work in your family?

What's missing?

A FRAMEWORK FOR EQUIPPING FAMILIES

Over the past few years, I have spent thousands of hours carefully researching how Christian parents are shaping their children's souls. Throughout this process, I've repeatedly bumped up against a painful but unavoidable

> "Parents don't realize the necessity and urgency of discipling their children."
> —Patricia Jones

truth: The overwhelming majority of Christian parents are not actively engaged in any sort of battle for their children's souls. When it comes to the process of discipling their progeny, most Christian parents—especially fathers—have abandoned the field.

If you as a parent are personally engaged in a process to transform the contours of your child's soul, you are a minority.

However, I envision a time when Christian parents consistently engage in planned discipleship processes with their children. I eagerly anticipate an era when children regularly experience family worship times and spontaneous spiritual conversations. These practices are not consistently happening in Christian households right now—I know that. But I believe that they can happen, and I firmly hope that they will.

That's why I've written this book. It is for present and future pastors, youth ministers, and children's ministers who are interested in shifting their ministries to equip families. It's also for parents and church volunteers who want to understand how to develop better partnerships between churches and homes. As you read this book, my first hope is that *you* will join me in the process of parental discipleship. No, I'm not expecting you to show up at the café while I disciple Hannah. I want you to carve out your own times and places to shape the souls of the children God places in your life. Once you and your family have caught this vision, I long for that same vision to spread to parents in your church and in other churches throughout the world.

WHAT THIS BOOK WILL NOT PROVIDE

I want to be up-front, though, and also let you know what I won't try to give you in this book. I have no plans to provide a quick fix that a youth or children's ministry can finish in a few weeks. What's more, I will not ask you to append one more program to a ministry calendar that's probably too packed already. (In fact, what I'm proposing could require you to cut a few programs!) What I will share in this book is not a plan for adding more programs but a process for reorienting the ministries that you're already doing.

A few years ago, I coined the phrase "family-equipping ministry model" to describe the framework for this process of reorienting existing ministries to partner with parents. Since that time, family-equipping has emerged as a distinct and identifiable approach to family ministry in many churches. This process can't fit in a box on the shelf of your local Christian bookstore because it isn't about a curriculum or event. It's about a lasting partnership between your ministry and the parents of the children and youth in your ministry. You can't purchase partnerships of this sort, and you can't cultivate them in precise time periods that a church calendar dictates. These partnerships require commitments to a long-term process, and they are likely to look different in every ministry context. They will require you to seek prayerfully how to live out God's calling in your particular ministry.

> "When I think of parents discipling their children, I can't help but think of my parents and how, as young Christians, they began home Bible reading. No one had given them any materials, they had not grown up in Christian homes, yet somehow they knew this was important. Why is this escaping Christian parents today? But my parents were probably the exception then, too. I don't know of any of my friends whose parents had devotions, even though my friends came from Christian homes."
>
> —Shyre McCune

At the same time, there are clear patterns that these partnerships have tended to follow as they have developed in different churches. The particular process I am proposing arises from a careful study of several ministries that have effectively called parents to engage actively in their children's spiritual development. It's my prayer that this framework will help you lead the parents in your church from abdication to active engagement in cosmic combat for their children's souls.

THE CURRENT STATE OF CHRISTIAN FAMILIES

At this point, you may be wondering, "How do you know that parents have really abdicated their role in the Christian formation of their children? Who knows? Maybe most Christian parents really are actively discipling their children, and you just don't know it!"

If that question has crossed your mind—and I hope it has!—you've raised a valid point. There are good reasons to be skeptical about claims like these. Far too many Christian organizations have tossed out far too many panicky alarms that have been based on sloppy statistical research.

That is not the case, however, when it comes to this research into parental disengagement from their children's spiritual lives. These observations are rooted in multiple research studies that reach far beyond my personal experiences. In 2007, the seminary where I coordinate family ministry programs partnered with an organization known as FamilyLife to develop better approaches to family ministry. One of the projects pursued by FamilyLife has been the Family Needs Survey.[1] This survey took a careful look at the needs and habits of churched families. The round of study that ended in 2008 included data from nearly forty thousand parents. This data has provided a statistically reliable snapshot of what is and what is not happening in Christian homes throughout North America. When it came to parental involvement in the discipleship of children, the results of the FamilyLife study were far from encouraging. According to the Family Needs Survey:

- More than half of parents said that their families never or rarely engaged in any sort of family devotional time. Of the minority that did practice some sort of family devotions, one-fourth admitted that these devotional times were sporadic.
- Approximately forty percent of parents never, rarely, or only occasionally discussed spiritual matters with their children.

- Nearly one-fourth of parents never or rarely prayed with their children; another one-fourth only prayed with their children occasionally.

FamilyLife Family Needs Survey

	Never or rarely	Occasionally	Several times a month	Several times a week	Almost daily
Pray with children (excluding mealtimes)	24 percent	25 percent	15 percent	13 percent	22 percent
Pray with spouse (excluding mealtimes)	52 percent	24 percent	9 percent	6 percent	10 percent
Talk about spiritual values with children	8 percent	30 percent	29 percent	22 percent	12 percent
Have family devotional time	56 percent	23 percent	8 percent	6 percent	7 percent

A few months ago, the Gheens Center for Christian Family Ministry at the seminary where I serve sponsored a more in-depth study with a smaller sampling of participants. The primary purpose of this study was to determine the precise dynamics of parents' disengagement from children's spiritual development. I oversaw this round of research—research that reinforced many of the findings from FamilyLife.

On the positive side, both studies suggested that around twenty percent of parents were praying, reading Scripture, and engaging in family devotions with their children at least once each week. Around one-fourth had read or discussed the Bible with their children seven or more times in the past couple of months.

The rest of the news was not so good, however. Our Family Discipleship Perceptions and Practices Survey revealed that:

- More than one-third of parents with school-aged children had never engaged in any form of family devotional or worship times at any time in the past couple of months. For an additional three out of ten parents, such practices occurred once a month or less.

- Among two-thirds of fathers and mothers, biblical discussions or readings with their children happened less than once each week.
- One in five parents never read, studied, or discussed God's Word with their children.

Remember: The parents surveyed in these studies were church attendees. Virtually all of them professed to be Christians, and they were involved in small group Bible studies. These numbers represent the rhythms of life in many core families in real-life congregations—parents who faithfully attend every week and serve in the church's ministries, teenagers who rarely miss their small group Bible studies, and children who are consistently present in Sunday school. Yet, in most of their homes, prayer with one another is infrequent at best. Times of family devotion and Bible study range from rare to nonexistent. From the perspective of one out of every five parents, church activities seemed to have been the family's sole intentional experiences of Christian formation.

Please don't mistake my point here. I am not suggesting that family devotions, Scripture studies, or spiritual discussions can somehow guarantee godly households. And yet, in the absence of such practices, it is difficult to see how parents can possibly be training their children to treasure God's Word or follow Jesus Christ with passion and joy. Cosmic combat for the souls of the rising generation swirls unseen around us even in our calmest moments. But with few exceptions, the parents in our churches have disengaged from the battle.

Family Discipleship Perceptions and Practices Survey
Discipleship Practices in Churched Households

	Never	Once	A couple of times	Three or four times	Five or six times	Seven or more times
Other than mealtimes, how many times in the past *week* have I prayed aloud with any of my children?	21 percent	11 percent	14 percent	13 percent	20 percent	21 percent
How many times in the past *month* have I read or discussed the Bible with any of my children?	20 percent	10 percent	25 percent	10 percent	9 percent	26 percent
How many times in the past *month* have I discussed any biblical or spiritual matters with any of my children while engaging in day-to-day activities?	7 percent	2 percent	21 percent	19 percent	20 percent	31 percent
How many times in the past *two months* has my family engaged in any family devotional or worship time in our home?	35 percent	10 percent	21 percent	6 percent	5 percent	22 percent

WHAT FAMILY MINISTRY IS AND WHY IT'S WORTH IT

The animated feature *The Incredibles* is a favorite movie in our household—and one of my favorite scenes is the family meal early in the film.

Dinner at the Parr household has deteriorated into sheer pandemonium. The infant squeals in delight at the chaos as his two siblings engage in superpowered combat with each other. A frazzled mom stretches and strains unsuccessfully to restore order.

And what about Bob Parr, father and former Mr. Incredible? He stands to the side, physically present, relationally absent, and utterly uncertain as to what to do. His sole advice thus far has been, "Kids, listen to your mother."

Finally, his wife flings a frantic plea in his direction: "Bob! It's time to engage! Don't just stand there. Do something!" And, to his credit, Bob Parr *does* try. The problem is, Mr. Incredible has no clue how to engage the situation wisely, and his engagement results in greater chaos.

Then, the doorbell rings.

Suddenly, everyone scrambles for a seat at the table and, by the time the door opens, what the visitor sees is a perfectly placid all-American family.

Many parents in your congregation have been walking in Mr. Incredible's shoes for a long time.

They have observed their children's spiritual development from a disengaged distance. They have watched youth and children's ministers stretch and strain to promote growth. And though we as youth ministers and children's

> "After decades on the back burner of congregational life, family ministry has suddenly become a hot topic. Type 'family ministry' into a search engine, and your computer is likely to crank out more than twenty-five million results in fewer than ten seconds."
> —Bryan Nelson

directors have tried to hide it from them, most of these parents have noticed that we *don't* have it all together. Still, they're watching, wondering if they should play a larger part in the discipleship of their families.

Now, in a growing movement in churches throughout the world, ministers are suddenly turning to these parents and shouting, "It's time to engage!" The problem is that many of them don't know how or why, and part of the reason is because we as church leaders aren't quite certain either.

WHAT *IS* FAMILY MINISTRY, ANYWAY?

> "As we examined our church context, here's what we concluded: In our well-intentioned efforts to reach students for Jesus Christ, we had developed ministry models that failed to call parents to embrace their role as the primary disciple-makers in their children's lives. The church had tacitly encouraged this parental abdication by relentlessly promoting benefits and life-changes that would accompany increased participation in ministry activities. As a result, the church and families were being split spiritually along too many key fault lines."
> —Jay Strother

In many churches, this call for parents to engage has taken the title of "family ministry." However, this is not the only meaning that's been ascribed to the family ministry—and that's part of the problem when it comes to engaging with parents. Church leaders aren't certain what they mean when they say "family ministry."

"Unlike other areas of ministry focus," Chap Clark has observed, "family ministry has emerged without any sort of across-the-board consensus of just what it is. . . . Because of this lack of a common perception of family ministry, people responsible for family ministry in churches are often confused and frustrated."[1] And no wonder! As many as four distinct meanings for "family ministry" can be found among contemporary churches: (1) In some churches, family ministry implies Family Life Education— a program for counseling troubled families or teaching intact families how to communicate more effectively; (2) some churches set the nuclear family at the center and focus all their efforts on developing healthy Christian households; (3) other congregations take family ministry to mean a program for developing family-like relationships in the church; and (4) still other congregations see family ministry as a catchall title to describe the separate programs that they offer for each member of the family. A few churches have no idea what they mean by family ministry—but the church down the street had a family ministry and it sounded like something that might attract more people, so these churches launched one too. Now, they're wondering what to do with it.

Family Ministry: The process of intentionally and persistently coordinating a ministry's proclamation and practices so that parents are acknowledged, trained, and held accountable as primary disciple-makers in their children's lives.

No wonder, then, that a prominent youth leader sent out this plea a few years ago for a practical definition of family ministry: "If someone knows a simple definition of family-based youth ministry, please send it right away. I've read (and enjoyed) most of the books written on the subject. In fact, I can still remember reading . . . *Family-Based Youth Ministry* the very week it was published. . . . However, I'm still looking for that simple definition and practical handle."[2]

So was I for several years.

In the end, I developed my own definition of family ministry based on ministry experience, research, and discussions with churches all over the world. My definition is less about a particular program and more about how we can redeploy the programs that we already have. Here's what I mean by family ministry: The process of intentionally and persistently coordinating a ministry's proclamation and practices so that parents are acknowledged, trained, and held accountable as primary disciple-makers in their children's lives.

I don't pretend that this definition somehow represents the final word on family ministry, but this understanding has been field-tested and refined by years of ministry and research with a wide variety of churches. This form of family ministry is not about any particular program or curriculum. It's about a process of equipping parents to engage actively in the discipleship of their children.

WHY NOT LEAVE THINGS THE WAY THEY ARE?

Here's one significant struggle you will face, though, if your ministry begins to prioritize parent-equipping: Many parents have no clue how to engage in their children's Christian formation. After all, in many churches, age-organized programs have claimed that task for a couple of generations. As a result, when you call parents to engage in their children's lives, things are likely to turn a little messy and confusing.

After decades of disengagement, many parents simply don't know what it means to function as primary faith trainers in their children's lives. Some parents may give up on discipling their children after their first family devotional ends in the emergency room because two children fought over who would read the Scripture and then chose to reenact David and Goliath in the living room, complete with a dishtowel slingshot and five smooth decorative stones. A few parents may confuse discipleship with hovering over everything that their child does. Other parents may ask, "If parents begin discipling their children, what are the children's and youth ministers supposed to do? Isn't that what we hired them for?"

The process of transitioning to family ministry will be difficult, perhaps even painful at times. At some point, you will ask yourself, "Is it worth it?

"Jesus once said to his disciples, 'Render to Caesar the things that are Caesar's, and to God the things that are God's' (Matt. 22:21 ESV). What was Caesar's was indicated by means of an image of Caesar stamped on the coin; the image of God is stamped on our children. As the shepherd of my family, I must constantly render my children to God. Anything less turns family ministry into one more borrowed strategy or program and will yield only short-term interest in the church—or no gain at all. If no attempt is made to partner with parents and to equip them to disciple their children, the very ministry structures that appear successful outwardly will sabotage authentic effectiveness."

—David Prince

In a recent study, it was discovered that Christian parents do not look primarily to God's Word for guidance in parenting. They primarily depend on how their own parents parented, and secondly on advice from friends. God's Word came in third place.[3]

WHAT FAMILY MINISTRY IS AND WHY IT'S WORTH IT

Does our ministry really need to shift? Why not just keep doing programs and activities like we've done them for decades?"

Your staff or volunteers may even challenge you with questions like, "Why are we doing this? What is the motive for these changes? And is that motive sufficient to make it worth the cost?" In those moments, you might find yourself wondering whether the motives that brought you to this place are sufficient to sustain such radical changes in your ministry model. I am convinced that the changes are worth the cost—but only if the church is making these changes with the right motives.

THE MATTER OF MOTIVES

In any ministry that seeks the glory of God more than the success of the organization, the motives for change are every bit important as the change itself. If right changes are made with the wrong motives, those changes typically don't turn out to be nearly as right as they seemed like they would. "All the ways of a man are [pure] in his own sight," Solomon once observed, "but the LORD weighs the motives" (NASB)—that is to say, God looks not only at outward actions but also at inward motives (Prov. 16:2). God sees our hearts, and his Word cuts through our hidden motives (Heb. 4:12–16). He calls us to pursue purposes that bring glory to his Son, and he pledges to disclose the motives of our hearts when Jesus returns (1 Cor. 4:5; 1 Thess. 2:4). That's why, before I present a process for transforming the patterns in your ministry, I want to take a careful look at why the church's ministries should change.

"Even active students receive only forty hours or so of biblical instruction each year from their churches. Parents, on the other hand, have more than three thousand hours a year in which they're constantly 'teaching' their children in some way! Our church recognized that—if we wanted to see an emerging generation that loves God with everything in them—we would have to redirect our ministry's time and energies toward equipping parents to impress truth in their children's lives day-by-day."
—Jay Strother

Put another way, as you read the next section of this book, I want you to ask yourself, "What is the right motive for pursuing family ministry in my church? What is the problem with prevailing practices? Why not simply leave things the way they are?"

In the process, you may find that the problem that you thought was the problem isn't really the problem at all.

WHAT TO LOOK FOR IN THE FIELD

Gap

THE KEY CONSIDERATION

How wide is the gap between what parents are doing and what they should be doing to disciple their children?

HOW TO FIND WHAT YOU'RE LOOKING FOR

Worksheet A: Family Discipleship Perceptions and Practices Survey

BEFORE YOU BEGIN

Communicate with key leaders in your congregation. Depending on your congregation's polity, the key leaders might include deacons, ministry staff, elders, or a senior pastor. Develop plans to assemble a team in your particular area of ministry to explore how the church can partner more effectively with parents. After gaining whatever approvals are appropriate in your congregation, assemble the team. In a larger congregation, this team might include staff and other key leaders. In a smaller congregation, this team may simply be a handful of vital ministry volunteers. Work to develop this team into a group that will champion family-equipping in the ministry that you serve.

WHAT TO DO

Make plans to meet at least monthly with the family ministry team. Enlist team members to assist in surveying the parents in the ministry that you serve, using Worksheet A: Family Discipleship Perceptions and Practices Survey. Once the data has been collected, summarize the results of the survey in a series of charts to provide a snapshot of how families are functioning when it comes to spiritual formation. Carefully compare what is actually happening in the families in your congregation with what should be happening. Where do you see causes for celebration? Where do you see a gap between what is and what ought to be? Which gaps will be the most difficult to close? Which one is most urgent to narrow as soon as possible?

WHEN TO DO IT

At least six months before you plan to begin the transition to family ministry

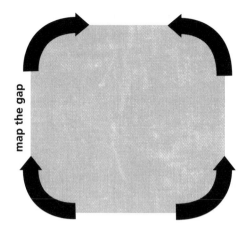

THINK ABOUT IT TOGETHER

Work through these activities with the family ministry team to develop a shared vision for your congregation's family ministry.

1. Study Ephesians 5:18—6:4, focusing on verse 4. The covenant relationship of a husband and wife is a divine mystery that God intends to reflect Christ's relationship with his church. Children are a fruit of this relationship. What did Paul present as the responsibility of Christian parents in relation to their children? Explore together the meaning of Paul's words in their original context.

2. Look at the results of the Family Discipleship Perceptions and Practices Survey from your church. To what degree are parents in your congregation living in obedience to Ephesians 5:18—6:4?

3. Watch the family dinner scene from *The Incredibles*. What do you see in this film clip that accurately reflects the families in your congregation? How do their perspectives and practices make it difficult for parents to engage in discipleship processes with their children? What practices in your church may unintentionally deepen family fragmentation instead of strengthening intergenerational appreciation?

4. As you consider emphasizing the responsibility of parents to function as primary disciple-makers in their children's lives, what makes you anxious?

What could go wrong? In the margins of this book, write each potential roadblock that your church could face. Every day this week, pray specifically and intentionally about each possible difficulty.

5. Begin asking simple, thought-provoking questions in your congregation to guide parents toward God's expectations—questions such as, "Who is primarily responsible to guide children toward the gospel? What do you think most Christian parents are doing to disciple their children? What is the most helpful thing that our church has done to partner with you as a parent? How could our church help parents do a better job in discipling their children? Does our church's schedule allow staff members enough free evenings each week to guide their own children's spiritual development?"

RESOURCES TO HELP YOU MAP THE GAP

Anthony, Michael and Michelle, eds. *A Theology for Family Ministry*. Nashville, Tenn.: B&H Academic, 2011.

Jones, Timothy Paul, ed. *Perspectives on Family Ministry: Three Views*. Nashville, Tenn.: B&H Academic, 2009.

Stinson, Randy and Timothy Paul Jones, eds. *Trained in the Fear of God: Family Ministry in Biblical, Theological, and Practical Perspective*. Grand Rapids, Mich.: Kregel Academic, 2011.

Wright, Steve with Chris Graves. *ApParent Privilege*. Raleigh, N.C.: InQuest Ministries, 2008.

FOUNDATION 2
RETHINK YOUR GOAL

WHY *NOT* TO DO FAMILY MINISTRY

"So, tell me," I ask, "why do you want to transition your church toward a family ministry model?"

The two ministry leaders I'm meeting with over coffee are good people. Both of them are passionate about the gospel, and they long to be faithful to Scripture. Their church has asked me to partner with the staff to minister more effectively to families. It's a midsized congregation, with two hundred or so people present each Sunday morning. I've completed the preliminary assessments, and fewer than one-third of parents in their congregation are consistently engaged in any form of discipleship or spiritual development with their children. This morning, we're convening at a café a few blocks from their church campus to map some initial changes.

"Well," the pastor begins "nine out of every ten kids are dropping out of church after they graduate, aren't they? Evidently, what we're doing right now isn't working."

The pastor is in his late twenties or early thirties. He graduated from a nearby denominational college a couple of years ago. The church recently called him as the pastor after the previous pastor retired. The church's leadership team is searching for a student minister, but for now, the pastor is leading the youth group too. From what I've heard, he's already gathered quite a crowd. He's considering seminary, but he's not certain he can handle the coursework with all the events that he has planned for the upcoming year. Summer camp is only two months away, so decisions about theological education will have to wait.

"Mm-hmm," the children's director agrees. She has overseen the children's programs for nearly two decades. For the first fifteen years or so, she led as a volunteer. A few years ago, her husband unexpectedly passed away. She needed a job to support herself and her teenage son, so the church's leadership turned her volunteer role into a paid position. Even in these early stages of the change process, her openness has been encouraging. Except for a janitor and a secretary, the pastor and the children's director are the church's only paid positions at this time. "Eighty-eight percent is what they said at the conference a few weeks ago. We just want to do so much better than that."

"Is your church actually losing that many?" I ask.

Both of them look at each other before shrugging.

"I—I don't really know," the pastor replies. "I mean, most of them, we don't see after they graduate. Sometimes that's because they're involved in another church or they've plugged into a college fellowship, I guess. Sometimes they move away. I don't think the church has ever actually done a survey or anything like that. It just seems to me that a lot of them *do* drop out."

The children's director nods and continues, "What we thought is that, if we had some programs to teach parents how to grow their kids spiritually, we could stop the dropouts before they happen."

"I want to help your church," I say to them. "And I will do everything that I can to help you. But first, I'm going to ask you to rethink your reasons for considering these changes. The problem that you think is the problem is probably not the problem at all."

THE INFAMOUS EVANGELICAL DROPOUT STATISTIC

Over the past couple of years, I've had conversations of this sort with hundreds of church leaders. The denominations have differed, the locations have spanned the globe, and the churches themselves have ranged from rural chapels to suburban megachurches. Yet the script inevitably runs something like this: Eighty percent, maybe even 90 percent, of students are dropping out of church after high school! Can you help us launch a family ministry program to fix this problem?

In these statements, ministers and church members are simply aping the conventional wisdom that they've heard at conferences and read in Christian books. According to these widely proclaimed assumptions, one of the most pressing ministry problems is the high percentage of students whose church involvement can't seem to persist more than a year past the pomp and circumstance of their high school processionals. A recent Internet search revealed nearly a quarter of a million references to the infamous evangelical dropout statistic.

This shocking dropout statistic represents a starting point for all sorts of demands for modifications in ministry practices—including the launch of family ministry programs. The logic throughout most of these references runs something like this: The standard for youth ministry effectiveness is retention of students beyond high school, and an overwhelming percentage of students are dropping out after high school. Therefore, current strategies for youth and children's ministries are clearly not successful. If only churches could come up with more effective ministry practices, they could fix the dropout rate and become more effective.

One author—in a self-proclaimed manifesto for the future of youth ministry—puts it this way:

> Kids are dropping out of church after youth group at staggering rates. . . . There are flaws in many of our assumptions and methods. . . . While our thinking was correct—for its time—the world of teenagers has changed. . . . When you're in a poor, rural country and see a horse-drawn wagon rolling down a dirt road, you think nothing of it. It fits. But when you're driving through Pennsylvania Dutch country and see a horse-drawn buggy rolling down a nice, paved road and holding up traffic, it seems as though something doesn't fit. In many ways youth ministry today is the latter horse-drawn buggy.[1]

In other words, the dropout rate demonstrates a flaw in our present practices, and our present practices are flawed because we haven't kept up with the times. If only we can come up with ministry methods that fit more effectively within the culture, we can fix the dropout rate—until, of course, the cultural gales gust in some other direction, and the latest trend turns into one more horse-drawn buggy.

> "Crying 'The sky is falling!' may sell books, but it never fixes problems."
> —Ed Stetzer

As I have consulted with congregations about family ministry, here's what I have found in many churches: Congregational leaders see family ministry as a quick counterbalance for the high dropout numbers that they've heard at a conference or read in a book. They perceive partnering with parents as a fix for the problem of a faith that can't seem to last past the freshman year of college.

IS THE SKY REALLY FALLING?

Perhaps you've read about the crisis too. Maybe you heard a speaker mention the dropout statistic at a recent conference. Perhaps that's even why you purchased this book: You're convinced that better partnerships between your ministry and parents might provide the perfect solution to dismal retention rates. If that's why you picked up this book, I commend your desire to partner with parents. At the same time, I want to challenge the logic that has brought you to this place. In fact, I want to make a suggestion that may seem a bit radical at first: The dropout rate is not a sufficient reason to reorient your ministry practices; in fact, the dropout rate may not be a problem at all.

Allow me to unpack what I mean by this: It's uncertain whether the rate of attrition that looms so large in our ecclesial anxiety closet even exists. And furthermore, even if a high dropout rate does exist, attrition rates represent an inadequate means for assessing ministry failure or success. Attrition rates are certainly not a sufficient motivation to swap ministry models—even if that means switching to a family ministry model. To understand what I'm suggesting, let's first take a closer look at the numbers behind the infamous evangelical dropout statistic.

GUT FEELINGS RARELY PROVIDE GOOD STATISTICS

In the first place, where did this data come from? When did conference speakers first begin to claim that the vast majority of youth were exiting the church before their sophomore year of college? And was their research reliable? The first references to the dropout statistic come from the late 1990s. That's when a well-meaning but statistically challenged speaker reported a post youth group attrition rate of 90 percent.

And how did he obtain this number?

When a persistent doctoral student tracked down the data, here's what the student found: The speaker's information was based on nothing more than the "gut feelings" that he gathered and averaged from a roomful of youth ministers.[2]

There's nothing wrong with asking a few people how they feel about an issue. Yet the communal hunch of a single group rarely results in a reliable statistic. In this case, an informal averaging of personal recollections resulted in a wildly overstated percentage that received tremendous publicity. As a result, over the past couple of decades, many youth ministries have leaped from one bandwagon to another, driven by the unsubstantiated guesses of a few youth pastors at one particular gathering in the waning years of the twentieth century. Another popular dropout figure—88 percent—has been traced back to the personal estimates of two youth ministry veterans.[3]

So, why do the dropout percentages represent an insufficient reason to reorient your ministry toward an emphasis on family ministry? In the first place, it's because many of these dropout numbers—particularly the nine-out-of-ten ratio—have little basis in fact. This infamous evangelical attrition

> "American evangelicals, who profess to be committed to Truth, are among the worst abusers of simple descriptive statistics . . . of any group I have ever seen. At stake in this misuse are evangelicals' own integrity, credibility with outsiders, and effectiveness in the world."
> —Christian Smith

rate does not rightly describe the present reality, and it probably never described any past reality.

So what is the real attrition rate? How many church-involved students actually do drop out in the months following their graduation ceremonies? The answer to this question depends largely on how you define church involvement. When involvement in a faith community is defined as attendance in the past seven days, the young adult dropout rate is around 38 percent. When church involvement is defined as two months of attendance at any time during the teenage years, about 61 percent of young adults disengage from church after high school. When a research sample mixes twice-a-month attendees with more involved young adults, the dropout rate rises to 70 percent. A few conservative evangelical megachurches have recently reported reliable retention rates of 88 percent or better among young adults who had been highly involved in dynamic student ministries that emphasized discipleship and missions—meaning that these congregations lost 12 percent or less of their young adults.[4]

And what are the factors that really do affect retention rates?

Parental involvement in a child's spiritual development is one highly significant factor—but there are other factors at work too. The earlier young adults marry, the more likely they are to remain involved in church. Some studies have also suggested that young adults tend to reengage with church by the time they turn thirty, perhaps around the time that they marry. If marriage is indeed a mechanism for reengagement in church, it is possible that the present problem of young adult dropouts results primarily from a postponement of marriage. In 1950, men typically married when they were almost twenty-three years old, now young men are waiting until they're twenty-eight to say "I do"; among women, the median age of first marriage has escalated even more radically, from twenty to twenty-six.[5] One result of this pattern may be a longer gap for many dropouts between disengagement from church and reengagement.

To be sure, even the moderated attrition patterns that I have reported here are not a cause for celebration. Yet the real dropout numbers vary widely, and they are affected by a range of factors that's far broader than family ministry. This much seems clear, though: The real numbers are far removed from the spurious statistics that have been spouted from the platforms of far too many ministry conferences.

Studies of Young Adult Dropout Patterns

Dropout percentages vary from one study to another. Although it is possible to question whether twice-per-month attendance is the best definition of "church involvement," the 2007 LifeWay Research study represents the most thorough research to date.

Who was included in the study sample?	What was the date of the study?	What was the dropout rate?
Church attendees and dropouts, with *dropout* defined as someone who once attended church but who has not attended church in the past two years (Roozen)	1980	46 percent dropped out at some point during their lives, with 15.5 percent dropping out in their teenage years and an additional 9.1 percent dropping out as young adults
Youth (ages 16–17) and young adults (ages 18–29), with *attendance* defined as attending a community of faith at some point in the past seven days (Gallup)	2002	38 percent dropped out from older youth (ages 16–17) to young adulthood (ages 18–29)
Young adults who had attended a church at least two months at any point during their teenage years (Barna)	2006	61 percent disengaged spiritually; no longer reading the Bible, praying, or attending church regularly
Young adults who had been involved in a church at least one year during high school, with *church involvement* defined as attendance at least twice a month (LifeWay)	2007	70 percent dropped out from early young adulthood (ages 18–22) to middle young adulthood (ages 23–30); of these dropouts, 35 percent returned to twice a month or more church attendance in their mid to late twenties; if *church involvement* is defined as attendance twice per month or more, the net loss from early young adulthood to middle young adulthood was 45 percent.

WHY JESUS WASN'T WORRIED ABOUT RETENTION RATES

The infamous nine out of ten dropout statistic was a false alarm. Most likely, your congregation loses far less than that, and about half of the dropouts return within a few years.

But let's suppose for just a moment that your ministry actually does have an abysmal attrition rate. What if your church really is losing nine out of ten attendees when they graduate from high school? Would that provide a sufficient motive to realign your congregation around an entirely new ministry model?

Here's another way of asking the same question: Is ongoing church involvement really the truest metric of a ministry's success? Or could it be that churches are using the wrong yardstick to measure their ministry models?

During his days on the dusty roads of Judea and Galilee, Jesus of Nazareth seemed to have been notoriously unconcerned about retention and attrition rates. At one point, "a large crowd" of well over five thousand was so wild about Jesus that they pursued him all around the Sea of Galilee (John 6:1–25). In contemporary terms, Jesus was well on his way to leading a megachurch. Then, after one particular teaching session, the numbers of paparazzi took a nosedive from several thousand to a single dozen—an attrition rate of well over 99 percent!

And what did Jesus say to the handful who remained?

"Okay, guys, what can I do to improve my retention rates? If I don't come up with a new ministry model, my Father will be so displeased with me! Let's brainstorm a bit to figure this out."

Not even close.

"Do you want to go away as well?" was what Jesus asked his closest companions as thousands of former followers filed away; then he added, "Did I not choose you, the Twelve? And yet one of you is a devil" (John 6:67, 70 ESV). A couple of years later, one Passover eve in the garden of Gethsemane, even the dodgy dozen deserted their Lord, and the divine dropout rate veered toward 100 percent (Mark 14:50; John 16:32).

At this rate, Jesus would likely have failed as a minister in many contemporary churches. Yet, in

Approximately 35 percent of young adults who drop out of church return within a few years. How has your congregation worked with parents to prepare them for the return of prodigal children? What resources might your church develop to help moms and dads engage in gospel-centered ways with children who have dropped out of church? How will your ministry help returning young adults to reengage with the congregation, calling them to repentance when needed but always reaching out to them with the grace of Jesus Christ?

all of this, the service of God the Son infinitely and perfectly pleased God the Father. Jesus remained the beloved one in whom the Father was well pleased (Mark 1:11; John 10:17). Even in the moments when his closest companions abandoned and denied him—in some sense, especially in those moments when "he was despised and rejected by men"—Jesus fully fulfilled his Father's will (Isa. 53:3–11). It was our sin that spiked Jesus to the cross, not his attrition rates.

So what's the problem with allowing retention rates to drive revisions in a ministry model? Simply that it turns the visible growth and maintenance of a local congregation into the primary focus instead of Jesus and the gospel. When retention rates determine how we envision a church's future, we have made too much of our own visionary ideals for the community of faith and too little of the One in whom we place our faith. Ministry leaders become visionary idealists seeking numeric gains rather than shepherds seeking to join in God's mission and to equip his flock. In the process, we lose sight of the true vitality and value of the very community that we were planning to preserve.

Please don't misread my point: The local, gathered community of faith is important. Jesus loves the church, and he gave his life to "present the church to himself in splendor" (Eph. 5:25–27 ESV). Whenever anyone drops out of active involvement in Christian community, the congregation is correct to be concerned! Yet neither numeric retention nor expansion can constitute a sufficient goal for reshaping a church's practices. Jesus is the paradigm for the growth of God's people (Phil. 2:5; Heb. 12:2). The church is the body of Christ, and the church's value and identity flow from the all-surpassing glory of Jesus (Eph. 4:12–16; Col. 1:24–27; 3:1–4). "Christianity means community through Jesus Christ and in Jesus Christ. No Christian community is more or less than this," German theologian

> "The man who fashions [his own] visionary ideal of community demands that it be realized by God, by others, and by himself. . . . When things do not go his way, he calls the effort a failure. When his ideal picture is destroyed, he sees the community going to smash. . . . Because God has already laid the only foundation of our fellowship, because God has bound us together in one body with other Christians in Jesus Christ, long before we entered into common life with them, we enter into that common life not as demanders but as thankful recipients."
> —Dietrich Bonhoeffer

Dietrich Bonhoeffer once wrote, "We belong to one another only through and in Jesus Christ."[6] The goal of the gospel is not a human ideal of retaining members in a visible community; the goal is to call people to Jesus. And so, the crucial question is not, "How many participants have we retained?" but "Who has glimpsed the truth of Jesus and the gospel in what we are doing?" Retention rates aren't the launching pad or the endpoint of God's plan; Jesus is (Rev. 22:13).

4

HOW TO FIND
THE RIGHT MOTIVATION

I heard clapping in the worship center and breathed a sigh of relief. I was waiting in the senior pastor's office for the final tally of ballots, and what I heard suggested that the vote had gone positively.

After six years as a pastor of a small church in rural Missouri, perhaps my life had grown too predictable. For reasons that weren't readily apparent at the time, God was moving me from the pastorate to youth ministry. It wasn't quite the move that I had anticipated as I completed degrees in ministry and divinity—but it was, without any doubt, God's direction. And I was confident that I would do well. I had, after all, taken classes in Christian education and youth ministry during the studies that led to my master of divinity degree. So I began the process of searching for a student ministry position.

A few months later, I found myself waiting for the results of a vote in this midsized congregation in Oklahoma. When I heard the applause, I rightly assumed that the position was now mine. My predecessor in this position had attracted sixty or more students each Wednesday evening and more than one hundred students each year for camp. Attendance on Wednesday nights had dropped into the twenties after the previous minister's departure, but everyone in the congregation seemed certain that as soon as they called a new youth minister, the numbers would race back to their previous peak and beyond.

When I walked out of the office, a host of smiling church members greeted me. More than a decade later, I can only recall the words of one well-wisher, however—and the reason that I remember his words is because they came back to haunt me many times in the months that followed. The words came from an older man known as Buck who walked with a limp and spoke with a smile.

"So glad to have you here, Brother Timothy," he said as he gripped my hand. "I know, with that guitar of yours, you're going to keep these youth here in our church—and bring in a lot more too. They're the church of the future, you know." With that, he hobbled down the long hallway, shaking hands with everyone he met.

Buck was one of the most faithful men in that congregation, and I still cherish Buck's contributions to the church and my ministry—but in that moment, Buck was wrong. He had bought into a vision for youth ministry that has driven untold numbers of student ministers to the brink of burnout and beyond. This false vision runs something like this: The purpose of student ministry is to gain and retain youth by entertaining them until the time comes for them to serve the church as an adult.

When that becomes the strategic foundation for a church's ministry, the standard for success becomes attendance and retention, and the central focus becomes finding the right ministers and methods to attract the highest numbers. The result of such a focus tends to be a frantic and unsustainable search for the latest hints and methods from the fastest growing ministries. Driven by this false standard for success, ministers become the ecclesial equivalents of the philosophers of Athens who were known to search incessantly for "something new" (Acts 17:21 ESV).

I must admit, however, that Buck's words felt good to me at that particular moment. I and my trusty six-string were like a congregational life

> "Inspired by parachurch youth ministries from the 1950s, . . . ministries of distraction keep youth moving from one activity to the next. . . . It's a Nickelodeon approach to youth ministry that seeks to appeal to kids' propensity for fun and recreation. . . . Like parents who pop in a video to entertain the kids when relatives arrive, the idea is to keep the young people from running out, to keep them in the general vicinity of the church, to keep them happy until they're mature enough to join the congregation."
> —Mark Yaconelli

insurance policy that would retain a rising generation of youth for the church's future. I quickly discovered that a loud guitar and a hunger for higher numbers simply weren't enough.

CHASING THE WRONG GOAL

On my first Wednesday evening at the church, I received my first hint that this task might be more difficult than I'd imagined. After a couple of games, I gathered the students for some high-energy worship songs, followed by a few slower choruses. Worship didn't seem to be part of what the students expected, but I persisted anyway. At the end of the musical set, I leaned my guitar against an amplifier, lifted my Bible over my head, and asked, "Okay, how many of you brought your Bibles?"

At first, no one responded.

And that's when he said it.

He was a senior in high school and five-year veteran of this particular youth group.

"This is Wednesday night youth group—we don't do Bibles here," he said. "And we don't come here to sing either. We're here to have fun."

Over the next few weeks, I persisted in my focus, and I discovered that this senior wasn't alone in his motivations for attending youth events. Numbers plunged into the low double digits. Parents complained to the pastor that their children weren't having enough fun. Church members—unaware that the previous minister's weekly youth group had frequently consisted of an hour of games and horseplay with a devotional tacked at the end—wondered why youth attendance on Wednesdays hadn't spiraled into the seventies and beyond.

I spent most of that first year torn between the conflicting expectations of the pastor, parents, students, and my own conscience. The pastor wanted greater numbers of youth and peace with the parents of these youth. The youth wanted a constant string of entertaining events. The parents wanted entertaining events too, but they also expected these activities, in some inexplicable way, to result in their children's spiritual

Gospel (from Anglo-Saxon *godspel*, "good story"; in Greek, *euangelion*, "good message"):
The gospel is the earthly life, death, and resurrection of God the Son, which accomplishes redemption and restoration for all who trust in Jesus and ultimately for the entire cosmos. Through his life, Jesus fulfilled God's law; he accomplished complete righteousness on behalf of sinners who have broken God's law at every point. Through his death, Jesus atoned for our sins, taking God's punishment for sin on his own self and obtaining forgiveness for all who would trust in him. Through his resurrection, Jesus vindicated his claim to be divine and guaranteed victory over sin and death through him. The saving work of Jesus not only redeems believing sinners, uniting them to God and to one another, but also assures the restoration of all creation. The gospel calls believers to join in God's work by proclaiming the gospel to all people and by seeking peace and restoration in their communities and in all creation. This is the "good story" and the "good message," that God redeems a fallen world by his grace.
Adapted in part from http://www.joethorn.net

maturity. From the perspective of many parents, I was the person that the church had hired for the tasks of discipling and entertaining their children.

What I did not recognize at the time was that the primary problem was not the students' desire to be entertained—that was merely a symptom. The problem was a deeply flawed model of ministry that I embraced even as I tried to move the ministry in a discipleship-focused direction. This faulty model places the professional minister at the center and makes gaining and retaining students the goal. In the case of student ministry, it turns youth group into a holding pattern for the church's future instead of calling students to live as servants of the gospel in their community of faith here and now.

But what if gaining and retaining numbers isn't the right goal in the first place?

And what if the center of the ministry isn't supposed to be the efforts of a pastor or professional minister? What if we centered every aspect of our ministry in the gospel and not in our efforts or methods? And what if we viewed Jesus Christ and his kingdom as the goal for our ministries? How might that change our expectations for ministries to children, youth, and families?

CHURCH GROWTH AND THE GOSPEL OF CHRIST

Sometimes, when a ministry makes much of Jesus and the gospel, the results do include numeric gains or stellar retention rates. Seven weeks after Jesus erupted alive from a garden tomb, three thousand women and men confessed Jesus as the risen Lord, and the congregation still kept growing (Acts 2:41–47). Before long, well over five thousand names could be found on the church scrolls (Acts 4:4). Even after two church members dropped dead while trying to bamboozle the apostle Peter, new believers still swarmed into the community (Acts 5:1–14). The earliest Christians rightly thanked God and recognized this growth as a glorious and wonderful outpouring of God's grace (Acts 2:47). And yet, gospel-centered proclamation of Jesus Christ doesn't always result in visible growth.

Sometimes, it may be possible to make much of Jesus with negligible results, at least as far as any human eye can see. The same Word of God that yields manifold fruit in one heart may be rejected as repulsive in another (Luke 8:4–18). The results of proclaiming God's truth could even include outcomes that seem negative from the perspective of retention rates (1 John 2:19). Furthermore, it is possible to attract and even retain a multitude of followers for all the wrong reasons (2 Pet. 2:1–2).

Yes, growth is part of God's good design for his cosmos (Gen. 1:11–12; 2:9) and for his church (1 Cor. 3:6–7; Eph. 2:21; 4:15–16; Col. 2:18–19; 2 Thess. 1:3). And yes, the proclamation of God's Word does result in growth and the fulfillment of God's purposes (Isa. 55:10–11), but this growth may take place in ways that are difficult to quantify in ratios of attrition and retention. Growth often unfolds less like a series of figures on a ledger sheet and more like seeds sprouting in the soil or like yeast seeping through a lump of dough (Luke 13:18–21). Godly growth is sometimes slow, often hidden, and frequently frustrates our dreams and designs. But it is always centered on Jesus and the gospel.

SKETCH THE SITUATION

What percentage of students in your church remain highly involved after high school?

How many become less involved?

How many switch to another church in the area?

How many move away and become involved in another church?

How many completely drop out of church?

Draw a pie chart to represent how many young adults in your church fit into each category. If necessary, add additional categories to depict the patterns in your particular congregation.

GOSPEL-CENTERED FAMILY MINISTRY

All of this has profound implications for why and how a church ministers to families. If the congregation's motive for forming a family ministry is to find a programmatic cure-all to solve a perceived problem of losing young adults, the strategy will have failed before family ministry even begins—even if every church member applauds the new program as a resounding success. Such a congregation has bought into the soul-draining delusion that growth depends not on the Word of God but on implementing the right programs to respond to each problem.

This sort of family ministry results, at first, in a rapid flurry of family friendly activities. Then, as soon as new problems and programs come along, the family events fade into the background as the newest quick fix takes center stage. Such patterns reflect much of the pragmatic consumerism of Western culture and little of gospel-centered community. According to the apostle Paul, the pagans of past cultures "exchanged the glory of the immortal God for images made to look like mortal man and birds and animals and reptiles" (Rom. 1:23). In our own way, we, too, trade the glory of God for the short-lived pleasures of lesser gods. Whereas the pagans exchanged divine glory for images of terrestrial beauty, we tend to substitute one more curriculum, one more series of steps to success, one more problem-solving program that eclipses the gospel.

Family ministry of the sort that I am describing in this book is not a program to fix a congregation's retention problems. It cannot be reduced to a series of conferences or activities or seminars. The kind of family ministry that I am envisioning is a movement toward equipping Christian households to function as outposts of God's mission in the world. Through family ministry, families become contexts where Christian community is consistently practiced with the goal of sharing the good news of God's victory far beyond our families. The gospel is rehearsed in families and reinforced at church so that God's truth can be revealed to the world. This isn't about retaining young adults on the attendance rolls; it's about coordinating families around a shared, Spirit-motivated perspective on parents and children.

"Where did we get the idea that training of parents should happen primarily through church programs with a bit of help from the pulpit? What if the training of husbands and fathers began to come more from relationships with other, more mature men? Jesus traveled, ate, taught, rebuked and did life with those who were most closely and intimately following him. But somehow we've gotten the idea, at church, that a few hours each week of structured lectures with some occasional focused programs can bring intimacy with Jesus and train people for life. Imagine if a husband only gave his wife three hours of personal time each week—and what if lectures were the primary means that he used to communicate? How much would their relationship grow? We don't need more programs; we need deeper relationships."
—Aaron Stevens

FINDING THE REAL PROBLEM

The coffee mugs are nearly empty. The morning rush is over and the café has grown quiet. My discussion with the two church staff members has been long but productive, yet both of them are still a bit skeptical. They came to me wanting to fix a perceived problem with retention, and my response has been that retention isn't even the real problem.

"That *sounds* good," the pastor says, "but I don't see how we can sell it to the church. I mean, if there aren't any problems with what we're already doing, why go to the trouble of changing things?"

"Whoa, whoa," I respond, waving my hand, "I'm not saying that there aren't any problems. What I'm trying to get at is that family ministry is not a program to fix retention rates—and that retention rates aren't the primary issue in the first place."

"Well, *is* there a problem with what's happening in our church families?" the children's director asks as she slips her mug into the tray of dirty dishes.

"Sure—and, even though retention rates aren't the real problem, it could be that some of the dropouts are a symptom of these deeper issues. Take a look."

Both staff members peer over my shoulders as I click through several charts that illustrate parents' lack of involvement in their children's spiritual development. Most parents in their church haven't even opened a Bible with their children in the past six months. Fewer than 20 percent pray with their children at any time other than meals. Fewer still practice any form of family devotions.

"So the problem is just that parents need to start reading the Bible and praying with their kids?" the pastor asks. "Because, if that's all that needs to happen, we could invite parents to youth group one Sunday night and train them to do family devotions. I could even make up some worksheets to help them."

"That's a good idea—it really is," I tell him. "But, if you want them to engage spiritually with their children for longer than a few weeks after the event that you're talking about, you'll need to build some foundations to make family ministry part of the culture. Getting parents to do faith talks or family devotions is a great start—but it's only a start. And, unless the culture changes too, parents won't make it a habit."

"I thought we were just launching a family ministry program," he slumps into his chair and crosses his arms. "Now, you're talking about changing our ministry culture—that's massive. I don't even know where we would start."

"Real change doesn't happen instantly; it takes time. And you start with something far more basic than what parents do with their kids."

"And that would be . . . ?" the query comes from the children's director.

"I think the parents in your ministry may need to learn who their children really are."

WHAT TO LOOK FOR IN THE FIELD

Goal

THE KEY CONSIDERATION

What goal is motivating your movement toward a family ministry model?

HOW TO FIND WHAT YOU'RE LOOKING FOR

Worksheet B: Motives Matter

WHAT TO DO

Gather your family ministry team. Work as individuals through the first part of the Motives Matter Worksheet, "Problem-Centered Planning: Developing Goals in the Wrong Direction," and compare your results. Discuss points of agreement and disagreement. Then, work as a group through the second part of the worksheet, "Gospel-Centered Planning: Developing Goals Based on God's Priorities." Work toward consensus on what belongs in each box under "Gospel-Centered Planning."

Based on the group's consensus, develop a tentative, one-sentence mission statement for the family ministry team.

WHEN TO DO IT

At least four months before you plan to begin the transition to family ministry

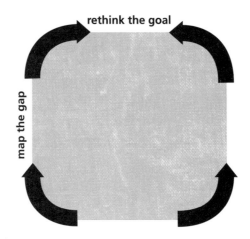

THINK ABOUT IT TOGETHER

Work through these activities with the family ministry team to develop a shared vision for your congregation's family ministry.

1. Carefully study Ephesians 4:10–16. In light of verse 16, what should shape and guide a church's growth? What forms might this growth take in your congregation?

2. In the past, what has typically motivated changes in ministry practices in your church? Prayerfully consider what may need to shift in your team's motivations for considering family ministry.

3. List every activity for youth or children that will happen this week in your congregation. What is the real goal behind each of these activities? Do these goals consistently reflect a clear plan for godly, gospel-centered growth?

4. How many of your ministry activities with children or youth recognize and celebrate the central role of Christian parents in processes of discipleship?

5. Is it possible that some of your ministry's activities with children or youth may actually be working against the primary role of parents in discipleship? If so, how?

RESOURCES TO HELP YOU RETHINK YOUR GOAL

Shields, Brandon. "Family-Based Ministry: Separated Contexts, Shared Focus." In *Perspectives on Family Ministry: Three Views*, edited by Timothy Paul Jones, 98–120. Nashville, Tenn.: B&H Academic, 2009.

Smith, Christian. "Evangelicals Behaving Badly with Statistics," Books & Culture. n. d. http://www.christianitytoday.com/bc/2007/janfeb/5.11.html.

Stetzer, Ed. "Curing Christians' Stats Abuse," *Christianity Today* (January 2010). http://www.christianitytoday.com/ct/2010/january/21.34.html.

Wells, David F. "Clerics Anonymous." In *God in the Wasteland: The Reality of Truth in a World of Fading Dreams*, 60–87. Grand Rapids, Mich.: Eerdmans, 1995.

FOUNDATION 3
FRAME YOUR MINISTRY IN GOD'S STORY LINE

DISCOVER WHO YOUR CHILDREN REALLY ARE

No matter how well-designed a seminary's curriculum may be, the bulk of a pastor's training still occurs in the crucible of ministry—which is why my role as a seminary professor rarely ends with the commencement ceremony. In the months following the mass bestowal of master's degrees in mid-May, I inevitably receive at least a few calls from students who have been freshly called to vocational ministry positions. Many of them want to stop by my office for a few moments to talk about a struggle or two, and I am blessed to be their sounding board.

This week, the call came from a recently minted master of divinity. He's the youth pastor in a larger congregation that has long relied on professionalized programs for the discipleship of children and youth. For most parents in the congregation, their role in their children's spiritual development begins and ends when they drop off their progeny at the church doors. This graduate has gotten the right message about the importance of family ministry, but he's impatient when it comes to implementation. Three months have passed since he and his wife moved into the parsonage, and he's already preparing to reorganize the entire youth and children's ministry.

The youth pastor shows up for our meeting a few minutes early, and it quickly becomes apparent that he wants advice about how to press the church toward the changes that he has already mapped out. In the first half-hour of our conversation, my suggestions were mostly, "Don't give up, but be patient. Learn to love the people and build the right foundations first."

"So how do I get the parents to do what they ought to do?" he asks with a touch of exasperation.

"First off, rethink your goal. The purpose isn't just to get parents to perform certain tasks. If that's your focus, you may add a few temporary good deeds to what the parents are doing, but you won't see any lasting transformation. It won't be long until the behaviors fade, and you'll be back where you started."

"What do the parents need then?" he persists.

"For one thing, parents need to see their children in light of the gospel. In some sense, parents don't know who their children really are."

It's nearly noon, and this fact provides the perfect excuse for us to continue our conversation at a local Mediterranean grill. The youth pastor offers to drive, so we clamber into his decade-old Ford Mustang, which is strewn with the physical artifacts of an active youth ministry. A stack of high-powered water blasters are entangled with a balloon launcher in the backseat. A couple of crumpled medical release forms are stuffed between the front seats. A half-dozen name tags from camps and conferences dangle from the rearview mirror.

"Parents need to find out who their children really are?" the youth pastor echoes my earlier words as he pulls his car out of the parking lot. "So I'm guessing what you want is for parents to spend more time getting to know their kids?"

"That wouldn't be a bad thing—but it isn't really what I'm getting at. What's the last novel you read?"

He looks at me quizzically before answering, "I don't really read novels—well, not anymore. Mostly youth ministry books, sometimes something on theology or leadership. When I was in eighth grade, I ran across *The Lord of the Rings* trilogy. I probably read those books twenty times. It's been years since I've read one of them, though."

"Let's suppose you only had the first book of the three, *The Fellowship of the Ring*. How satisfying would the story line have been?"

"Well, I can guarantee you I wouldn't have read the trilogy that many times! If you only had the first part of the story, you'd miss . . . well, almost everything. The one ring would never make it to Mount Doom, Sauron would never be destroyed, and Aragorn would never become king. I think I would have had to write my own ending just to keep my sanity."

"Exactly," I say. "But it would be just as frustrating if you only had the last volume or the middle one—then, you'd have no clue why the characters are doing what they do. For a story to make sense, it has to have a beginning, middle, and end. You need all three acts."

"Are we still talking about parents and their kids?" he asks.

"Sort of," I pause for a moment. "We're living in a story; a true story. It's God's story. There are different acts in God's story too."

He perks up, "Let me guess: creation, fall, redemption, and consummation? See, I did learn something while I was at seminary."

"Good to hear," I smile. "That story line should shape everything we do as believers in Jesus Christ. The problem is, many parents don't see their responsibilities as parents in light of the whole story of God. A lot of the time, they see their responsibilities in light of creation and fall, but they don't understand how redemption and consummation apply in their households—and those acts are essential to the gospel. Parents are working with only part of the story in place."

"Okay, so what does all this have to do with parents understanding who their kids really are?" he asks as he parks.

"Everything," I assure him. "When the whole story of God frames every part of a family's existence, parents don't just see their children as sons and daughters. They also see their children as potential or actual brothers and sisters in Christ. When parents see their children not only as their children but also as their brothers and sisters, it changes everything."

TELLING THE SAME OLD STORY

Accused by a member of Parliament of always reiterating "the same old story," British Prime Minister Margaret Thatcher once retorted, "Of course, it's the same old story. Truth usually is the same old story."[1] Whatever one may think of Margaret Thatcher's politics, her words mesh well with biblical theology.

For believers in Jesus Christ, the same old story of God's work in human history is what continually reveals the truth about our world and us. It is through this story that God forms, reforms, and transforms our lives.

GOD'S STORY LINE

Creation: God created the cosmos and positioned Adam and Eve as vice-regents to rule and care for his world (Gen. 1:26–31). By establishing limitations on humanity's choices, God demonstrated that he remained the sovereign ruler and king of the universe (Gen. 2:15–16).

Fall: Adam and Eve sinned and ceased to subject themselves willingly to God's reign. God exiled the first family from Eden and revealed his plan to redeem and reign over humanity through the offspring of Eve (Gen. 3:15–24). The story of Israel is the story of God's preservation of the people through whom he would bring this royal seed into the world.

Redemption: Through Jesus the Messiah and King, God broke the power of the curse that resulted from the fall and of the condemnation that came through the law (Gal. 3:10–14). Through his suffering on the cross, Jesus endured God's wrath in the place of sinful humanity (Rom. 5:9–11). Through his resurrection on the third day, Jesus demonstrated his royal triumph over death—a triumph that, though already real and true, will not be fully realized or recognized until the end of time (1 Cor. 15:20–28).

Consummation: In his own time and way, God will consummate the reign that Jesus Christ, the "King of kings" (Rev. 19:16), has already inaugurated. The city of God will descend to earth, God himself will dwell among his people and make all things new (Rev. 21:1–5).

At the center of the story stands this singular act: In Jesus Christ, God personally intersected human history and redeemed humanity at a particular time in a particular place. Yet this central act of redemption does not stand alone. It is bordered by God's good creation and humanity's fall into sin on the one hand and by the consummation of God's kingdom on the other. This is the story that Christians have repeated to one another and to the world ever since Jesus vanished through the eastern sky, leaving his first followers gap-mouthed on a hill outside Jerusalem (Acts 1:9–12). This same story of creation, fall, redemption, and consummation should frame every aspect of our lives—including family life.

Unfortunately, in many contexts, the foundational framework for family ministry has not been creation, fall, redemption, and consummation.

Instead, the motivating narrative for family ministry has been a series of dismal retention numbers that may not even reflect the real patterns in that particular congregation. But family ministry rooted in such transient whims and temporary hype will never have a lasting impact. Lasting impact must find its foundation in a plotline that's far richer and deeper than the latest statistic—the story of creation, fall, redemption, and consummation. In this divine story line, we glimpse the truth about who children are, who parents are, and how they should relate to one another.

GOD'S CREATION AND HUMANITY'S FALL

The plot is a familiar one—a creation filled with goodness, a serpent filled with lies, a woman gazing at forbidden fruit, and the man silent by her side. A choice was made, a hand was extended, and suddenly all that had been so good was contorted into sin, sorrow, and death. No one on earth today has ever stood in the spot where our primeval parents took their first taste of cosmic treason. Yet our souls still bear the scars of that ancient exile from Eden.

There is both good news and bad news for families in these early acts of God's story. The good news is that families and children are not byproducts of humanity's sin. The divine design for marriage and parenthood preceded the fall (Gen. 1:28). Even now, by raising children, men and women exercise divinely ordained dominion over God's creation. This is pleasing to God (Gen. 1:26–28; 8:17; 9:1–7; Ps. 127:3–5; Mark 10:5–9). Parents provide for their families and nurture their offspring. This too is part of God's good plan (Matt. 7:11; 1 Tim. 5:8). Parents train their children to avoid what is evil. Appropriate discipline is also godly and good (Prov. 13:24; 19:18; 29:17; Heb. 12:5–9).

But there is bad news for families too. Because of the extent of humanity's fall, meeting children's needs and bettering children's behaviors will never be enough. At best, parental patterns of provision and discipline prepare children to know the kindness of a heavenly Father, to sense the depth of their own sin, and to recognize their need for the gospel. At worst, these patterns train children to be satisfied with regulating outward actions and with pursuing gains that cannot persist past the end of time.

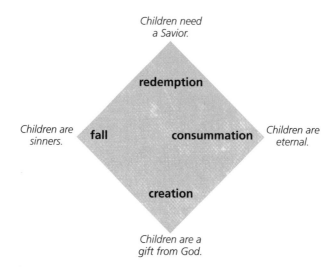

REDEMPTION ACCOMPLISHED, CONSUMMATION GUARANTEED

Viewed from the vantage of creation and fall, children are both gifts to be treasured and sinners to be trained. And yet, no amount of training can ever raise a child to the level of God's perfect standard. Every order of creation, including parenthood, has been subjected to frustration with the gap between the glory of God's creation and the fact of humanity's fallenness (Rom. 8:20–22). And so, as Jesus dangled from the splintered beam of a Roman cross on that fateful afternoon, God himself bridged the gap between his perfection and humanity's imperfection (2 Cor. 5:21). The death of Jesus brought about redemption in the present; his resurrection guaranteed the consummation of God's kingdom in the future.

REMEMBERING WHO YOUR CHILDREN REALLY ARE

This truth introduces a radical new dimension to family life. To embrace God's redemption is to be adopted as God's heir, gaining a new identity that transcends every earthly status (Rom. 8:15–17; Gal. 3:28–29; 4:3–7; Eph. 1:5; 2:13–22). What this means for followers of Jesus is that our children are far more than our children; they are also potential or actual brothers and sisters in Christ.

Husbands and wives, parents and children, men and women, widows and orphans, the plumber's apprentice and the president of the multinational corporation, the addict struggling in recovery and the teetotalling grandmother—all of us who are in Christ are brothers and sisters, "heirs of God and co-heirs with Christ" (Rom. 8:17; see also Gal. 4:7; Heb. 2:11; James 2:5; 1 Pet. 3:7).

Seen from this perspective, my relationship with my children takes on a very different meaning. These daughters whom I adore will remain my children for this life only. I am the father of Hannah and Skylar until death, but—inasmuch as they embrace the gospel—I will remain their brother for all eternity. Put another way, if your children stand beside you in the glories of heaven, they will not stand beside you as your children (Luke 20:34–48) but as your blood-redeemed brothers and sisters, fellow heirs of God's kingdom.[2] Remember the words of Jesus? "Whoever does the will of my Father in heaven is my brother and sister and mother" (Matt. 12:50). Paul echoed this perspective when he directed Timothy to encourage "younger men as brothers" and "younger women as sisters, with absolute purity" (1 Tim. 5:1–2).

Does this mean that once a child becomes a brother or sister in Christ, the relationship of parents to children somehow passes away? Of course not! The gospel doesn't cancel roles that are rooted in God's creation. Jesus and Paul freely appealed to the order of God's creation as a guide for Christian community (Matt. 19:4–6; Mark 10:5–9; Acts 17:24–26; 1 Cor. 11:8–9; 1 Tim. 2:13–15). Paul called children in the redeemed community to respect their parents (Eph. 6:1; Col. 3:20; 1 Tim. 5:4). Meaningful labor was present before the fall and persisted in God's plan even after the fall (Gen. 2:1–15; 2 Thess. 3:6–12). Far from negating the order of God's creation, the gospel adds a deeper and richer dimension to the patterns in the first act of God's story.

GLIMPSING A DIMENSION DEEPER THAN CREATION AND FALL

What does this truth mean for the day-to-day lives of parents in our churches? As a parent, I am responsible to provide for my daughters and to prepare them for life; as an elder brother, I am called to lay down my life for them (1 John 3:16). As a parent, I help Hannah and Skylar to see their own sin; as their brother, I am willing to confess my sin (James 5:16). As a parent, I speak truth into their lives; as a brother, I speak the truth patiently, ever seeking the peace of Christ (James 4:11; 5:7–9; Matt. 5:22–25; 1 Cor. 1:10). As a parent, I discipline my daughters to consider the consequences of poor choices; as a brother, I disciple, instruct, and encourage them to pursue what is pure and good (Rom. 15:14; 1 Tim. 5:1–2). As a parent, I help these two girls recognize the right path; as a brother, I pray for them and seek to restore them when they veer onto the wrong path (Matt. 18:21–22; Gal. 6:1; James 5:19–20; 1 John 5:16).

Because I fully expected that Hannah would one day embrace the gospel, I began developing the habits of a brother long before our first conversation about what it means to follow Jesus. Because I anticipate that Skylar is moving toward becoming a follower of Jesus, I do the same with her here and now. I did all of this imperfectly; I still do. I fall far short of living as a parent, spouse, and fellow heir within my family—and so will you. The central point is not that you or the members of your church will perform these deeds perfectly. It is, instead, that family members embrace the gospel more fully and begin to view one another in a renewed way, as brothers and sisters participating together in the "grace of life" (1 Pet. 3:7).

Children are wonderful gifts from God—but they are far more than that. Viewed from an eternal perspective, every child in a household is also

> "My biggest frustration in youth ministry was that I could never seem to spend enough time with the youth to effect lasting change. The best and brightest students, I had for three or four hours a week. Many of the students, I had for only an hour each month. 'If only I could be around them more!'—that was what I kept thinking. So I coached, I taught, I tutored, just to spend more time with the youth. Then I became a parent, and I realized that God had already designed a way around this problem of not having enough time with students to be the catalyst for change in their lives. That role wasn't mine in the first place. It belonged to their dads and moms."
>
> —Josh Remy

a potential or actual brother or sister in Christ. Until parents perceive their children in this way, they fail to see who their children really are.

WHAT HAPPENS WHEN PARENTS SEE WHO THEIR CHILDREN REALLY ARE

So what happens when parents perceive their children as potential or actual brothers and sisters in Christ? The writings of Paul provide some hints. The same apostle who called Timothy to encourage younger believers as Christian brothers and sisters also commanded fathers to nurture their offspring "in the discipline and instruction of the Lord" (Eph. 6:4 ESV; see also Col. 3:21).

In other letters, Paul applied these same two terms—*discipline* and *instruction*—to patterns that characterized the disciple-making relationships of brothers and sisters in Christ. *Discipline* described one of the key results of training in the words of God (2 Tim. 3:16). *Instruction* implied guidance to avoid unwise behaviors and ungodly teachings (1 Cor. 10:11; Titus 3:10). Such texts strongly suggest that Paul was calling parents—and particularly fathers—to do far more than manage their children's behaviors and provide for their needs. Paul expected parents to engage personally in teaching their children God's words and ways. Summarizing these words from Paul, a fourth-century pastor known as John Chrysostom said to fathers in his congregation, "Never regard it as a small matter that your child should be a diligent learner of the Scriptures."[3]

HOW PAUL KNEW WHO YOUR CHILDREN REALLY ARE

These expectations were not unique to Paul. When Paul penned these words, he was drawing from a Scripture-saturated legacy that had shaped the Hebrew people for centuries. This ancient heritage of songs, statutes, and ceremonies foreshadowed the coming of Jesus and explicitly recognized the primacy of parents in the formation of their children's faith.

When Moses received the law of God, he passed on precise instructions regarding how the people should preserve these precepts: "You shall teach them diligently to your children" (Deut. 6:6–7; see also 11:1–12; Ex. 12:25–28). Moses assumed that children would ask their parents about the family's spiritual practices, and he commanded fathers to be prepared to instruct their children about the Lord's mighty deeds (Ex. 12:26–27; Deut. 6:20–25; see also Josh. 4:5–7). Part of the purpose of the yearly Passover celebration was to remember as a family the story of Israel's redemption (Ex. 13:14–22).

In the prologue to his proverbs, one of Israel's ancient sages reminded youth to learn divine wisdom in the context of their homes: "Hear, my son, your father's instruction, and forsake not your mother's teaching" (Prov. 1:8 ESV). Even in the songs of Israel, parents were called to impress on their children the stories of God's works. A songwriter named Asaph put it this way: "I will utter dark sayings . . . that our fathers have told us. We will not hide them from their children. . . . [They will] arise and tell them to their children, so that they should set their hope in God" (Ps. 78:2–4, 6–7 ESV). Perhaps most important of all, a primary evidence of the in-breaking of God's kingdom—predicted by the prophet Malachi, proclaimed by John the Baptist, and consummated in the presence of Jesus Christ—was that, in believing households, the hearts of children and fathers would be turned toward one another (Mal. 4:6; Luke 1:17).

WHAT ABOUT THE COMMUNITY OF FAITH?

This is not to suggest that the community of faith has no role in the discipleship of children. After all, the fulfillment of Malachi's predictions in the ministry of Jesus included the recognition that the unity of the Christian community runs deeper than any physical kinship (Matt. 12:46–50; Luke 14:26). Blood may be thicker than water, but the bond of the Spirit is weightier than either one—and God intends this spiritual bond to grow among his people until the entire earth is clothed in glory divine (Hab. 2:14; Rev. 5:9–14). That's why every believer is called to pursue this deeper bond with every other human being, calling the faithless to faith in Christ and discipling less mature believers (Matt. 28:18–20; Acts 5:42; 8:25; 14:21).

And where should these processes of evangelism and discipleship begin? With those who are nearest to us.

That's what the church father Augustine of Hippo was hinting at when he suggested, "Since you cannot do good to all, pay special regard to those who, by the opportunities of location, time, or circumstance, are brought into closer connection with you," knowing that God himself is at work in placing these persons near to us.[4] When it comes to discipleship, personal proximity is more important than any particular ministry program.

And who are the nearest unbelievers or young believers to Christian parents? Typically, they are our own children. And so, parents are called to actively engage in their children's spiritual formation not in spite of, but precisely because of the deeper kinship that is available through the Holy Spirit. The possibility of this deeper kinship calls parents to see their children not only as their children but also as potential or actual brothers and sisters in Christ.

God's creation and humanity's fall have positioned parents as providers and disciplinarians. Through redemption and consummation, parents are called to become disciple-makers as well. Because God has chosen to place particular children in close proximity to us, these disciple-making processes should begin with our own children.

God's calling does not end with the rehearsal of the gospel in our own households, though. The proclamation of the gospel that begins in our households should spill out beyond the confines of our homes, into our communities, and then to the uttermost parts of the earth (see Acts 1:8; 2:39; 26:20). And it all begins when parents begin to see who their children really are.

> "The person in your house that claims your first and nearest attention, is, undoubtedly, your wife; seeing you are to love her, even as Christ hath loved the Church. . . . Next to your wife are your children; immortal spirits whom God hath, for a time, entrusted to your care, that you may train them up in all holiness, and fit them for the enjoyment of God in eternity. This is a glorious and important trust; seeing one soul is of more value than all the world beside. Every child, therefore, you are to watch over with the utmost care, that, when you are called to give an account of each to the Father of spirits, you may give your accounts with joy and not with grief."
> —John Wesley

THE SPLIT IN GOD'S STORY LINE

Some tasks are more about skills than relationships. Tasks like fixing a faucet that is spewing water across the kitchen, for example, or setting a fractured femur are more about skills. The process of dealing with such crises may be more pleasant if you happen to know the plumber or the physician personally. Yet your greatest question is not whether you'd invite this individual to join your family on a coast-to-coast road trip. Your concern is whether this person possesses the professional skills to fix the problem. When a task is mostly about skills, it's typically a good idea to call in a trained expert.

In other areas of life, skills and training may be helpful, but the personal relationship matters more than the professional skills. Think of it this way: Suppose I called my wife this afternoon and announced, "Honey, guess what? Remember how you asked about a date tonight? Well, I hired a professional dater to take you to dinner and a movie. That's right, dear: a professional. He's much more skilled at dating than me; plus, since I'll be at home watching *Star Wars* with Hannah and Skylar, we won't even need to find a sitter. Have a great time."

If such an evening seemed even remotely interesting to my wife, she and I would have more problems than any date—professional or otherwise—could fix. In fact, if I seriously suggested such an evening, I suspect that many frosty nights would pass before my wife requested a date with me again. That's because, even though certain skills may be beneficial in your relationship with your spouse, marriage has more to do with a personal relationship than with expert skills. Certain people may equip you for better relational practices—but no one else possesses the proper qualifications to carry them out. How such tasks are done is significant, but who does them is far more significant.

> "What if part of the reason that parents in church aren't good at discipling their children is because parents aren't good at being disciples? You can't share what you don't have."
> —Tony Kummer

It's also that way when it comes to parents and the discipleship of their children.

Certain skills may be helpful in a child's Christian formation—but, when it comes to parents discipling their children, the task is not primarily about the skills; it's about a divinely designed relationship. The church may remind me to engage spiritually with my daughters. Ministers, elders, or deacons might even equip my wife and me to disciple Hannah and Skylar more effectively. Yet no one possesses the proper qualifications to undertake this task in our place because no one else can lay claim to the title of our daughters' father or mother.

Why, then, have so many parents—even Christian parents—abdicated their role in matters of salvation and spiritual growth?

Why do parents fail to see their children as potential or actual brothers and sisters in Christ?

And why is it so difficult for parents to begin the practices with their children that will enable them to see their lives in light of redemption and consummation?

THE UNSPOKEN MESSAGE

Of course, the primary reason for each of these shortcomings is that the fall of humanity affects every part of life—including family life. Sin perverts our capacity to rightly perceive reality. As a result, parents need guidance from God's Word and his people to see who their children really are. Many parents aren't discipling their children because they have never been discipled. They've never learned how the gospel applies in their every-day lives, including their parenting practices.

But there are also human means by which this distortion has developed over the past couple of centuries. One of these human means can be sum-marized in a single sentence: Churches have presented moms and dads with the impression that active participation in the discipleship of children is optional for parents.

Of course, no one has explicitly told parents that they shouldn't guide their children in light of redemption and consummation. What many churches have done instead is to develop comprehensively seg-mented programs for the evangelism and discipleship of children, all while rarely (if ever) even mentioning the role of parents in discipling their children.

In such congregations, processes related to redemption and consum-mation—including the function of disciple-making brothers and sisters in Christ—no longer seem to require the involvement of parents. The parental role in discipleship begins and ends when parents drop off their children at the church building. Parents, locked into the story line of creation and fall alone, do not discipline their children in ways that aim them toward the gospel. Instead, discipline disintegrates into mere management of external behaviors. The focus of parenting shifts away from the gospel and toward goals of personal happiness and material success.

The Christian formation of each generation takes place in age-focused groupings that isolate children and youth from other family members and generations. Youth groups serve as the disciple-making communities for middle school and high school students, while children's programs play this role for elementary students.

The unspoken message has been that the task of discipleship is best left to trained professionals. Schoolteachers are perceived as the persons responsible to grow the children's minds, coaches are employed to train children's bodies, and specialized ministers at church ought to develop their souls. When it comes to schooling and coaching, such perspectives may or may not be particularly problematic. When it comes to Christian formation, however, this perspective faces an insurmountable snag: God specifically calls not only the community of faith but also the parents to engage personally in the Christian formation of children.

This is one set of responsibilities that, from the perspective of Scripture, parents simply cannot surrender to someone else. When fathers and mothers hand over these tasks to the church, they lose sight of who their children really are. Parents see their sons and daughters as their children. But, in their practices of parenting, they miss the gospel-rich movements of redemption and consummation that are crucial to God's story; in the process, they lose sight of who their children really are.

The story line in Christian households has grown too small. The role of parents has been reduced to dealing with their children only in light of creation and fall. As a result, they fail to train their children as actual or potential brothers and sisters in Christ.

The real problem in all of this is not primarily about results or retention rates. The deeper problem has to do with an incomplete appropriation of the story of God in Christian families. When the whole story of God frames a family ministry, the result is not one more set of activities. The result is a gospel-centered, Scripture-grounded, Spirit-compelled partnership that equips fathers and mothers to participate personally in the discipleship of their children.

Family ministry is essential, but it must be far more than a colorful program that mingles two influences to increase the odds of getting better results. Such surface-level perspectives may improve a few passing symptoms, but they can never heal the underlying problem of a story line that is far too small.

THE SPLIT IN GOD'S STORY LINE

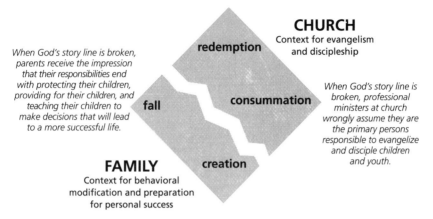

When God's story line is broken, parents receive the impression that their responsibilities end with protecting their children, providing for their children, and teaching their children to make decisions that will lead to a more successful life.

redemption

CHURCH
Context for evangelism and discipleship

consummation

fall

When God's story line is broken, professional ministers at church wrongly assume they are the primary persons responsible to evangelize and disciple children and youth.

FAMILY
Context for behavioral modification and preparation for personal success

creation

SKETCH THE SITUATION

Look carefully at the image "The Split in God's Story Line" above. Where in your ministries do you most clearly see this split between the role of the parents and the role of the church? Look at this month's church calendar. Where might each activity for children or youth fit on the image? In other words, does the activity relate more to: (1) appropriating the common grace of creation and coping with the effects of the fall, or (2) living out God's present work of redemption and looking forward to God's future work of consummation? Place each activity in the most appropriate place on the image. Now carefully and honestly answer these questions: (1) How many of the activities that relate to redemption or consummation also directly involve parents? (2) How many of these activities involve only youth or children and the ministry leaders for that age-group in isolation from parents? (3) What does this tell you about the ministry practices and priorities in your congregation?

PARENTING WITH YOUR GRANDCHILDREN IN MIND

My lunchtime meeting with the recent seminary graduate is over and now we're headed to his car.

"Can I be honest with you about something?" he asks, glancing down as he grinds his sandal sole against a blade of grass that's straining through a crack in the sidewalk.

"I certainly hope so."

"I have two boys—one who is five; the other one is seven—and I'm not doing anything consistent to disciple them. I don't know how many times I've started trying to do family devotions, but it only lasts a week or two before I get too busy and quit. When it all comes down, I guess I want to make these changes at church for me as much as anyone else. Maybe, if I can get the whole church on board, I'll finally start doing it too. But honestly, I just feel so nervous and inadequate every time I try to lead a family devotion. I can preach to a youth group all day, but I can't seem to share the gospel in my own family."

The lights in the walk signal switch from scarlet to white, and the two of us scuttle across the street. I am tempted to switch into my professorial mode and provide a list of practical pointers for family discipleship, but that response would give the false impression that I've somehow transcended the struggles that he has described. I haven't. What he needs to hear is the raw and honest truth.

"Me too," I respond.

"You too what?"

"I've done this for years, and I still feel inadequate sometimes. Don't give up—but don't expect changes in the church to be the catalyst that changes your home, and don't expect it to happen all at once. Truth be told, after my wife and I adopted our first daughter, it took us a couple of years to develop the habits that I practice and teach now. I should have started when Rayann and I got married, but I didn't. And honestly, there are aspects of family faith talks and discipleship that still make me nervous sometimes." We stop beside the Mustang as he fumbles with the keys. "And sometimes, I dread family faith talks because I have to admit that I haven't been practicing what I'm about to teach my family. It means that I need to confess my failures to my family and ask forgiveness—but that's also why these times are so important as we rehearse the gospel in our household."

"So I'm not the only one who feels this way?" the youth pastor sighs and smiles across the roof of the car as I shake my head. "What kept you going, then—you and your wife—when you were starting this in your family?"

I open the car door before responding: "Partly because I saw that this isn't something that Scripture presents as an option; it's something that God expects and that faithfulness to his Word demands. But there was something more than just recognition of God's expectations. I started thinking beyond this generation. I began parenting with my grandchildren in mind."

"Parenting with grandchildren in mind?" he asks as we slide into our seats and he starts the engine.

"There's a psalm that talks about teaching God's story to your children in such a way that

> "Why aren't parents discipling their children? Parents are busy, they feel inadequate, they have few models to imitate, and they are chasing idols, so they buy the lie that the church should do it for them."
>
> —Brian Haynes

'children yet unborn' [Ps. 78:6 ESV] pass the same truths to their children. When I pray with my girls, when I intentionally guide their spiritual formation, I am not thinking just about their growth and sanctification—though that's important too. My plan is that, a hundred years from now, there will be great-great- and great-great-great-grandchildren who can't imagine these practices not happening in their households, because I have so thoroughly ingrained them in my children's lives here and now. For those parents and children, my name will be long forgotten; I'll be nothing more than a footnote in the family tree and a gravestone in Cave Hill Cemetery. But I want God's Word to be so deeply engraved in my family that those future generations will not be able escape its implications. I hope to start something in my family that I cannot finish, because it will outlast my time on this earth."

"That's a lot bigger than reorganizing the youth and children's programs."

"Yeah—and a lot harder too," I admit. "And organizational changes may still be needed. But reorganizing the youth and children's ministries isn't the point. Take your time; work on training parents to see their children in light of God's story, and partner with someone who will hold you accountable too."

"I get the point. I'll keep you posted about how things are going," he says as we pull into the seminary parking lot. "But why is this so hard—teaching God's ways in your own household?"

"It's never been easy. Christian households are places where the gospel is practiced and proclaimed. That makes them targets of every power of darkness. Even in the decades after the New Testament books were completed, it's clear that some Christian families were failing to disciple their children. But, over the past few years or so, there have been a couple of primary culprits in this abdication."

"And those culprits are?"

"Time and training. Families have grown too busy to take the time, and church ministries have taken over the discipleship of children instead of training the parents. In most churches, it's become a matter of time and training. But, for you, the solution doesn't begin with a dissertation on the history of family discipleship. It begins tonight with two boys."

And so, we take the time to plan together how one husband and father will begin the process of partnering with his wife to guide two boys in light of God's story. Family ministry begins small and slow, but even the tiniest steps matter.

FOUNDATION 3
FRAME YOUR MINISTRY
IN GOD'S STORY LINE
FIELD GUIDE

WHAT TO LOOK FOR IN THE FIELD

God's story line

KEY CONSIDERATION

How do your congregation's ministry practices prepare parents to see their children in light of God's story line, as potential or actual brothers and sisters in Christ?

HOW TO FIND WHAT YOU'RE LOOKING FOR

Worksheet C: Living in God's Story Line

WHAT TO DO

Using Worksheet C: Living in God's Story Line, consider with the family ministry team whether your ministry practices tend more (1) to prepare parents to see their children in light of God's whole story line, or (2) to separate parents from engagement with their children in the movements of redemption and consummation. Carefully consider how you might change any ministry practices that separate parents from involvement in the movements of redemption and consummation.

WHEN TO DO IT

At least two months before you plan to begin the transition to family ministry

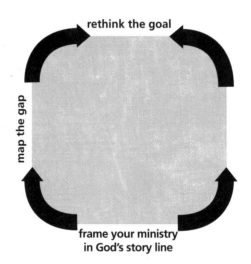

THINK ABOUT IT TOGETHER

Work through these activities with the family ministry team to develop a shared vision for your congregation's family ministry.

1. Lead an in-depth study of God's story line based on some or all of these biblical texts: Genesis 1:26–28; 18:16–19; Deuteronomy 6:4–9; Psalm 78:1–8; Romans 8:22–30; Ephesians 6:1–4; and Malachi 4:1–6.

2. Discuss how God has called parents to particular responsibilities that relate to each movement in the divine story line.

(a) In creation, God called humanity's primeval parents to fill the earth with children who would reflect God's image (Gen. 1:26–28).

(b) After the fall, God chose Abraham "that he may command his children and his household after him to keep the way of the LORD" (Gen. 18:19 ESV) and commanded Israelite parents to train their children in God's ways (Deut. 6:4–9; Ps. 78:1–8).

(c) Through faith in Jesus Christ, parents and children are adopted together as fellow heirs with Jesus and with one another (Matt. 12:50; Rom. 8:22–30). God has called the parents in the community of the redeemed to nurture their children in his ways (Eph. 6:4).

(d) In preparation for the consummation of God's kingdom on "the great and awesome day of the LORD," the prophet Malachi called for the hearts of fathers and children to be turned toward one another (Mal. 4:5–6 ESV).

3. List several events and activities in your church's ministries with children and youth. How might these ministries shift to partner more effectively with parents?

4. When parents see their children only in the framework of creation and fall, they tend to point their children toward better behaviors and successful lives. But they fail to see their practices of parenting in light of the grace, accountability, community, and eternal perspective that the gospel brings. Do the parents in your congregation view their practices of parenting in light of the gospel? If not, how can you guide them toward gospel-centered parenting?

5. What practices in your congregation might imply to parents that tasks related to redemption and consummation are best left to professional ministers or trained volunteers at church? Prayerfully consider how God might work through you to change these assumptions.

RESOURCES TO HELP YOU FRAME YOUR FAMILY MINISTRY IN GOD'S STORY LINE

Chester, Tim and Ed Moll. *Gospel-Centered Family: Becoming the Parents God Wants You to Be*. New Malden, Surrey, U.K.: The Good Book Company, 2010.

Farley, William. *Gospel-Powered Parenting: How the Gospel Shapes and Transforms Parenting*. Phillipsburg, N.J.: P&R Publishing, 2009.

Goldsworthy, Graeme. *According to Plan: The Unfolding Revelation of God in the Bible*. Downers Grove, Ill.: InterVarsity Press, 2002.

Plummer, Rob. "Bring Them Up in the Discipline and Instruction of the Lord." In *Trained in the Fear of God*, edited by Randy Stinson and Timothy Paul Jones. Grand Rapids, Mich.: Kregel Academic, 2011.

FOUNDATION 4
GIVE PARENTS THE GUIDANCE THEY NEED

WE'RE SUPPOSED
TO DO THAT AT HOME?

"You mean, we're supposed to do that at home?" she asked, staring wide-eyed at the video screen.

At the time, I took these words as nothing more than a passing question from a curious church member. In retrospect, her words represented far more than an inquiry about the contents of the video. What I was hearing was a crucial hint that should have opened my eyes to why Christian parents have disengaged from their children's spiritual development.

"No one ever told me how to do anything like that before." Would it be possible for a parent in your ministry to make a similar statement? If so, what does this suggest about your congregation's commitment to equipping parents to disciple their children?

Several months earlier, I had preached through Paul's letter to Ephesus. In the process of working through the sixth chapter of Ephesians, I introduced a practice that seemed quite simple and straightforward to me: At the end of every sermon, the last slide provided a short outline for parents to follow when leading their families in a devotional time each week. Week after week, I encouraged every family to designate one evening for a family devotional—nothing complicated, just a prayer, an activity, a biblical text, and a few discussion questions that related to Sunday's sermon. Most weeks, parents also received a printed handout with an expanded outline to follow at home.

Five months later, a church member waited at the back of the worship center while I spoke with some visitors after the morning message. She and her husband had been faithful members and servants in the church for several years. Their oldest child had recently professed faith in Jesus Christ. I assumed that she wanted to touch base with me regarding her child or perhaps about an event that her committee was planning. As the last visitors left the worship center, she approached me, gesturing toward the devotional guide on the screen.

And that's when she asked: "You mean, we're supposed to do that at home?"

I nodded, "That's why it's up there every week."

"Wow," she stared at the screen for several seconds. "No one ever told me how to do anything like that before."

Her tone wasn't unpleasant or even unwilling. Yet it was clear that a family devotional time was utterly alien to her thinking. I might as well have asked her to ride a unicorn to the moon. It had taken five months of outlines for her even to recognize that I seriously thought families might do this. She had been a church member since childhood, in three different churches at different stages of her life. And yet, confronted with the idea of faith training at home, her response was, "No one ever told me how to do anything like that before."

> Among the first followers of Jesus, believing households were contexts for the teaching of believers and for the evangelism of unbelievers (Acts 2:46–47; 5:42). Are the homes of believers in your congregation contexts for evangelism? Encourage faithful families in your church to commit themselves to inviting an unbeliever or an unbelieving family to their home for dinner at least once per month, with the goal both of building an authentic relationship and of gaining an opportunity to share the gospel.

WHAT I MISSED ABOUT FAMILY MINISTRY

At the time, I assumed her perceptions were the exception. To be sure, not all the parents in our church were actually doing what they ought to be doing, but surely, they at least knew what was supposed to be done. As far as I could tell, the problem was that parents had decided that professional ministers ought to be the primary faith trainers in their children's lives. With this assumption in mind, what I offered parents were many appeals but few clear instructions, a multitude of assumptions but no comprehensive plan.

I was wrong.

I was wrong about the solution to the dilemma. Emotional appeals from the pulpit may drive parents to engage in a few external practices for a week or two, but such responses will never lead to lasting transformation. What parents need is neither guilt nor gimmickry but a deeper rootedness in the transforming power of the gospel of Jesus Christ.

Furthermore, merely getting families to engage in devotions or discipleship practices isn't even the right goal in the first place. The goal of family ministry is for parents to see themselves and their families in light of the gospel. Certain habits and practices will inevitably result from such a vision. But defining family ministry in terms of these external practices will never develop well-discipled families. A focus on outward habits leads instead to well-heeled Pharisees who either flaunt their own counterfeit righteousness (Matt. 23:27–28; Luke 18:10–12) or who feel trapped by the recognition that they can never quite measure up to God's righteousness (Rom. 7:18–24).

> "It took my husband and me too long to realize that we were depending on the church and Sunday school to teach our kids. When I tell other people about our family devotions, I am asked all kinds of questions about how we do ours and advice on how they can get started. I am amazed at the number of families that don't read the Bible together or even have a simple bedtime prayer with their child—all because we let a busy life get in the way. How will our children ever know unless they see us do it and unless we are there to do it with them?"
>
> —Angie Berry

By God's grace, these truths became clear to me through the Scriptures while I was still serving as a pastor. But it was more than merely the solution that I had misconstrued.

I also missed the mark when it came to the question of why parents weren't engaging spiritually with their children—this, even after glimpsing the centrality of the gospel in parenting. I thought that, if parents weren't at least trying to engage spiritually with their children, it was primarily because they were in denial about their role. It was parents who had wrongly identified the discipleship of children and youth as the rightful domain of professional ministers—at least, that's what I assumed.

And that's where I was wrong once again.

WHAT PARENTS KNOW ABOUT THEIR ROLE

This assumption was still firmly imprinted in my mind when I partnered with a cluster of churches to discover the precise dynamics of parents' desertion of discipleship processes in their households. In this carefully designed study sponsored by the Gheens Center for Christian Family Ministry, congregations were selected to present a clear and accurate snapshot of parents in evangelical churches. And, on several key points, the results differed radically from what I had expected.

Here's what most surprised me: Parents did not view professional ministers at church as the people primarily responsible to grow their children's souls. In a radical reversal of my earlier assumptions, the overwhelming majority of parents identified themselves as the persons primarily responsible for the spiritual development and discipleship of their children. Parents knew that they were responsible for their children's spiritual growth.

> "For my family, it has been several generations since the men had an active, vibrant relationship with Jesus. My dad was content just to get me to church a couple times a week. His dad did the same thing—with an iron fist. Fathers [in my family] have taken their children to church, and they have been somewhat religious, but they haven't engaged personally in their children's spiritual development. I hope to break that cycle. I want to be involved in my son's growth as a Christian."
> —Aaron Stevens

Well over 90 percent of parents rejected the notion that professional ministers were the people primarily responsible for their children's spiritual development. When asked whether parents ought to engage personally in a discipleship process with their children, not one parent disagreed, and most parents strongly agreed. Fewer than 14 percent of parents expressed even the slightest agreement with the suggestion that church ministries are where children ought to receive the bulk of their biblical teaching. More than 90 percent of parents wanted to answer their children's biblical and theological questions. Only 1 percent of parents strongly identified church leaders as the persons who ought to develop their children's souls.

Despite my early prejudices in the opposite direction, the data compelled me to admit that most parents in evangelical congregations recognize their disciple-making role in their children's lives. They are fully aware that the spiritual development of their children is not a task that should be subcontracted to age-focused ministers.[1]

It's at this point that a paradox emerges, though. Even as parents admit their responsibility to function as primary faith trainers in their children's lives, most are doing little, if anything, to fulfill this role. For most parents, intentional processes of spiritual formation with their children range from sporadic to nonexistent. One out of every five parents admits to never engaging in practices of prayer, Bible reading, or worship in their households.

Family Discipleship Perceptions and Practices Survey
Parental Perceptions of Spiritual Responsibility

	Strongly disagree	Disagree	Somewhat disagree	Somewhat agree	Agree	Strongly agree
The church is where children ought to receive most of their Bible teaching	26 percent	45 percent	17 percent	10 percent	2 percent	1 percent
When my child spontaneously asks a biblical or theological question, I really wish that my child would have asked a minister or other church leader instead of me.	61 percent	31 percent	3 percent	2 percent	2 percent	2 percent
Parents, and particularly fathers, have a responsibility to engage personally in a discipleship process with each of their children.	0 percent	0 percent	0 percent	4 percent	34 percent	62 percent
Ministers or other church leaders are the people primarily responsible for discipling my children and teaching them to share the gospel with others.	37 percent	44 percent	11 percent	6 percent	0 percent	1 percent

Do you see the dilemma that emerges from this data? If more than 90 percent of parents see themselves as personally responsible for their children's Christian formation, why are so few of them doing anything consistent to disciple their offspring?

Of course, far more is involved in the answers to these questions than a few personal or organizational issues. What we are talking about here is cosmic combat. "Spiritual forces of evil in the heavenly places" are warring against parents' efforts to bring up their children "in the discipline and instruction of the Lord" (Eph. 6:4 ESV; see also v. 12). The sole sufficient response to such conflict is to clothe ourselves in the strength of God himself (Eph. 6:13–20).

At the same time, it is wise to recognize that the Enemy uses terrestrial trends and tools in this spiritual battle. Based on the research that was undertaken for this book, two specific factors seem to be blocking the pathway that leads toward consistent practices of discipleship in Christian households.

LACK OF TRAINING, SHORTAGE OF TIME

Now, I don't expect you to be a statistical specialist to understand this research—but I do want you to understand the significance of these two factors that I am about to present to you. The correlation between these factors and parents who had disengaged spiritually from their children was strong and highly significant. In this particular study, what this meant in practical terms was that one or both of these factors directly correlated with parental disengagement more than 90 percent of the time, and there was less than a 5 percent chance that this inference is incorrect.

So what are these two top factors in parents' failure to disciple their children? The primary point of resistance was that churches weren't training the parents. The secondary reason was that parents weren't making the time.

It was a matter of training and a matter of time.

A MATTER OF TRAINING AND A MATTER OF TIME

PARENTS AREN'T MAKING THE TIME

Parents in your ministry don't have time to disciple their children—or, at least, that's the way many of them feel when they look at their weekly to-do lists. Nearly half of the parents in the survey had resigned themselves to the notion that, to some degree, their families were simply too busy to engage in practices of family discipleship.

Two-thirds of parents admitted that family devotions or worship times were not a priority in their schedules. And what were the factors that prevented these parents from having the time for intentional spiritual formation in their households?

For a significant minority of parents, it was children's sports and school activities that trumped family time when it came to scheduling priorities. Nearly one-third of parents agreed that they were willing, at some level, "to do whatever it takes" for their children to succeed in certain sports or school activities.

And what if the resulting schedule was so hectic that it prevented the family from eating any meals together during the week? As long as the payoff at the end included academic or athletic successes for their child, these parents were willing to pay the price.

MORE THAN A GIFT FOR THIS LIFE

This pattern suggests that a significant number of parents in our ministries have allowed their priorities to be shaped by the dominant culture—a culture wherein the primary goal of parenting is to produce children who become happy, well-paid adults.[1] Parents perceive accomplishments in sports and schooling as their children's pathway to present popularity and future financial success. As a result, athletics and academics define these parents' designs for their children's lives.

> "Instead of asking parents to give their children a fancy education in secular literature . . . Paul asks the Ephesian laypersons, many of whom . . . were engaged in the ordinary occupations of this life, that they should educate their children in every doctrine and counsel of the Lord. Overseers and pastors ought to take note of this."
>
> —St. Jerome

These fathers and mothers see their children as gifts to be treasured—and this is good. In God's creation design, children *are* a blessing and reward (Gen. 1:28; Ps. 127:3–5). And yet, seen in light of the whole story of God, children are far more than a gift for this life.

If children were nothing more than a gift for this life, a single-minded focus on children's happiness and success might make sense. As long as the family's frantic schedule secures a spot for the child in a top-tier university, forfeiting intentional spiritual formation for the sake of competitive sports leagues and advanced placement classes would be understandable—if children were a gift for this life only. Perhaps working around the clock would be plausible provided that your children's friends are visibly impressed with the house you can barely afford. If children were a gift for this life only, maybe it would make sense to raise them with calendars that are full but souls that are empty, captives of the deadly delusion that their value depends on what they accomplish here and now.

But children are far more than a gift for this life. They are bearers of the gospel to generations yet unborn. In God's good design, your children and mine will raise children who will in turn beget more children. How we mold our children's souls while they reside in our households will shape the lives of children who have yet to draw their first gasp of air (Ps. 78:6–7).

Your children and mine are also eternal beings whose days will long outlast the rise and fall of all the kingdoms of the earth. They and their children and their children's children will flit ever so briefly across the face of this earth before being swept away into eternity (James 4:14). If our children become our brothers and sisters in Christ, their days upon this earth are preparatory for glory that will never end (Dan. 12:3; 2 Cor. 4:17—5:4; 2 Pet. 1:10–11). That's why our primary purpose for these children must not be anything as small and miserable as success. Our purpose should be to leverage our children's lives to advance God's kingdom so that every tribe, every nation, and every people group gains the opportunity to respond in faith to the rightful King of kings.[2]

"For what does it profit a man to gain the whole world and forfeit his soul?" Jesus asked his first followers (Mark 8:36 ESV).

When it comes to our children, we might ask a similar question: What does it profit our child to gain a baseball scholarship and yet never experience consistent prayer and devotional times with us, the parents? What will it profit our child to succeed as a ballet dancer and yet never know the rhythms of a home where we are willing to release any dream at any moment if we become too busy to disciple one another? What will it profit the children all around us in our churches to be accepted into the finest colleges and yet never leverage their lives for the sake of proclaiming the gospel to the nations? What will it profit pastors to lead the largest churches with the greatest discipleship programs if they don't disciple their own households?

There is no profit in such endeavors—no real or lasting profit, anyway—but the costs are painful, infinite, and eternal.

> "For what end do you send your children to school? 'Why, that they may be fit to live in the world.' In which world do you mean—this or the next? Perhaps you thought of this world only and had forgot that there is a world to come; yea, and one that will last forever! Pray take this into your account, and send them to such masters as will keep it always before their eyes. . . . Surely, if you love or fear God yourself, this will be your first consideration: 'In what business will your son be most likely to love and serve God? In what employment will he have the greatest advantage for laying up treasure in heaven?' I have been shocked above measure in observing how little this is attended to, even by pious parents! Even these consider only how he may get most money; not how he may get most holiness! . . . Upon this motive they fix him in a business which will necessarily expose him to such temptations as will leave him not a probability, if a possibility, of serving God. O savage parents! Unnatural, diabolical cruelty—if you believe there is another world."
> —John Wesley

HOW SUCCESS BECOMES AN IDOL

In the beginning, God infused humanity with a yearning for eternity (Eccl. 3:11). If the scope of our vision for our lives or for the lives of our children shrinks any smaller than eternity, our thirst for eternity will drive us to attempt to fill the emptiness with a multitude of lesser goals and lower gods—including the fleeting happiness and success of our children. When the happiness and success of children becomes the controlling framework for life, parents expect their children to have, do, and be more than anyone else, and they are willing to sacrifice family relationships and discipleship to achieve this objective. The result is a culture of childhood royalty that treats children like princes and princesses instead of potential or actual brothers and sisters in Christ.[3]

I am not suggesting that successes in academics, athletics, or vocation somehow stand outside God's good plan. Learning and play are joys that God himself wove into the very fabric of creation. Although cursed in the fall, work was also part of God's good design before the fall (Gen. 2:15; 3:17–23).

And yet, whenever any activity, however good it may be, becomes amplified to the point that no time remains for family members to disciple one another, a divinely designed joy has been distorted into a hell-spawned idol. God calls us, just as he called our father Abraham, to be willing to release every longing for our child's pleasure and success for the sake of obedience to God's Word (Gen. 22:2–18). In this, what God asks of us is no less than what he himself has already done in Jesus Christ: "He . . . did not spare his own Son, but gave him up for us all" (Rom. 8:32).

DOING LESS SO THAT PARENTS CAN DO MORE

Most parents in churches typically do believe, at least on the surface, that their children's existence will persist past this life. The problem is that this tenet of faith doesn't always make its way into their daily practices of prioritizing household commitments. Parents mentally accept the fact that their children will exist forever, but they do not live in light of this truth. When this truth works its way into daily life, parents begin to weigh their family's priorities and schedules in light of the gospel. Until the gospel drives even our scheduling priorities, families will continue to default to the values of the culture around them, and parents will remain too busy to engage in intentional discipleship with their children.

So how can your ministry help parents rethink their family's priorities in light of the gospel?

A critical look at your own ministry calendar is probably the best place to start.

The cluttered family calendars that hang from refrigerator doors in members' homes mimic patterns that are modeled each week in the church bulletin. Both tend to be excessively busy—and sometimes because of a similar fixation on visible success. Parents seek success for their children in the form of higher SAT scores or athletic victories; church leaders add more activities to make members happier and to improve the numbers on their annual church profiles.[4] The idolatry is the same; only the paperwork is different.

When ministry calendars become too crowded, weekly Bible studies, committee meetings, and youth groups compete with seasonal activities and monthly events. Eventually, families become so busy doing church that no time remains for them to be the church in their homes and communities. If your church is planning for parents to disciple children, your ministry may need to do less so that parents have time to do more. After all, if active church members invest half their evenings each week (or more), enabling their church's fixation on programs, where will they find the time to form the spiritual lives of their children? And when will they mentor children whose parents aren't yet believers?

Not only parents but also church ministries must be challenged to reevaluate every time commitment in light of God's plan for the homes of

Look at your church calendar for the past month. Consider carefully whether church activities may cause families in your congregation to be too busy. Then examine the schedule for your particular area of ministry. What activities could be merged with other activities, perhaps in partnership with another ministry in the church? How might some activities and events look different if you reshaped each one not only to engage a particular age-group but also to develop intergenerational relationships and equip children or youth to engage with their parents? If Christian parents in your congregation functioned as primary disciple-makers in their children's lives and in the lives of children whose parents aren't believers, which activities might become unnecessary? How might you redevelop existing activities to equip parents for this role?

his people. Over time, family ministry may require you to streamline, combine, and even cut back activities so that families become free to join God's mission in their households and communities.

This matter of time is highly significant, but scheduling priorities are not the sole roadblock in parents' practices of discipleship. Around half of the parents in the survey identified themselves as too busy to engage in practices of family discipleship—a significant proportion, to be sure, but not enough to explain the full number of parents who have disengaged from their children's spiritual formation. The second and far more significant problem has to do with the expectations and equipping that parents receive through their churches.

Family Discipleship Perceptions and Practices Survey Parental Scheduling Priorities						
	Strongly disagree	Disagree	Somewhat disagree	Somewhat agree	Agree	Strongly agree
I want to do whatever it takes for my child to succeed in certain sports or school activities—even if that means my family is too busy some weeks to eat any meals together.	16 percent	27 percent	26 percent	21 percent	10 percent	1 percent
I would like to do regular family devotions or Bible reading in our home, but my family is just too busy for that right now. It will probably be that way for quite a while.	8 percent	27 percent	17 percent	32 percent	12 percent	5 percent
I prioritize consistent family devotional or worship times in my family's schedule.	5 percent	33 percent	17 percent	23 percent	18 percent	5 percent

CHURCHES AREN'T TRAINING PARENTS

"No one ever told me how to do anything like that before," she said as she pointed at the video screen. As I think back, I see that she was right. As her pastor, I had urged parental involvement in children's spiritual development. I had lamented and even lambasted the lack of commitment to family discipleship. Yet I had never clearly shown parents how to engage personally in discipling their children—or even precisely what I expected them to do. And, as I thought about it, no church or ministry leader had ever equipped me to engage spiritually with my child either. What I was doing at that time to disciple my daughters, I did because I vaguely recalled bedtime prayers with my mother that continued into my teenage years, as well as daily Bible readings at the breakfast table when I was a child.

I wish I could write this off as an exceptional pattern that was limited to my own experience, but I can't. When the survey data from parents and churches came back, it became quite clear that my experiences were far from unique. As a whole, churches are not consistently encouraging or equipping parents to engage intentionally in their children's spiritual growth.

Family Discipleship Perceptions and Practices Survey
Parental Perceptions of Equipping for Family Discipleship

*For the purposes of this survey, "church leader" included pastors, elders, ministers, deacons, teachers, or small group leaders.

	Strongly disagree	Disagree	Somewhat disagree	Somewhat agree	Agree	Strongly agree
My church has helped me to develop a clear plan for my child's spiritual growth.	18 percent	41 percent	17 percent	18 percent	6 percent	1 percent
	Never	Once	A couple of times	Three or four times	Five or six times	Seven or more times
How often in the past year has any church leader* made any contact with me to help me to engage actively in any of my children's spiritual development?	68 percent	12 percent	14 percent	5 percent	0 percent	2 percent

WHAT PARENTS AREN'T GETTING AT CHURCH

When asked whether their churches had helped them to develop any plans for their children's spiritual growth, nearly 60 percent of churched parents disagreed or strongly disagreed, while an additional 17 percent somewhat disagreed. Only 7 percent could state without any reservation that their churches had helped them to plan for spiritual growth in their children's lives. When asked if any church leader had ever contacted them to help them to engage actively in their children's spiritual development, more than two-thirds of parents could not recall a single instance in the past twelve months.

Other recent studies have replicated these patterns: In a survey of churched parents with children under the age of thirteen, 81 percent said that no church leader had ever spoken to them about how parents could be involved in their children's spiritual development. A study of student ministry values and practices revealed that, when youth ministers' efforts and expenditures were analyzed, almost nothing was being done to equip parents to engage spiritually with their teenagers. Despite placing family ministry fourth on their lists of ministry priorities, youth ministers spent only 3 percent of their time and less than 3 percent of their budgets in any ministry that related to parents and families.[5]

All of this, despite clear evidence that most parents in churches want to be equipped to guide their children's spiritual development. When asked about their family's most pressing needs, more than three-fourths (77 percent) of church-involved moms and dads specifically mentioned their desire to know how better to help their children to grow spiritually. The same percentage of parents also wanted to be better equipped to teach Christian values in their homes.[6] And so, the issue seems to be not so much that parents have resigned their role as primary disciple-makers. It isn't even that parents don't desire to disciple their children. In most cases, the problem is that churches are neither expecting nor equipping parents to disciple their children.

PROVIDING WHAT PARENTS REALLY NEED

Sometimes, the truth hurts worse than you thought it would.

Hannah was in first grade when she asked the inevitable question: "Daddy, is Santa Claus real?"

I should have anticipated my daughter's question. As Christmas approached, her classmates chattered constantly about Santa Claus—but our family never mentioned the red-suited saint. I would like to claim that I had some profound theological rationale for my silence. Mostly, it was because, if I'm going to spend that much on Christmas gifts, I want my child to know that *I* wrote the check, not Mr. Claus. All of which probably explains why my child was a bit skeptical when her friends claimed a chubby old man would take a tumble down our chimney on Christmas Eve.

"Is Santa Claus real?" I mused. "Well, sort of. A long time ago, Nicholas of Myra was a pastor in a place that's now known as Turkey." And so, I told Hannah the true story of the benevolent bishop known as St. Nicholas who provided dowries for poverty-stricken girls. When I finished the tale, Hannah's eyes were a bit glazed, but she seemed to have gotten the point.

"So where's St. Nicholas now?" she asked.

"Well, he's in heaven now, I suppose. He died in the fourth century. A few years before he died, a Roman emperor locked him in a dungeon. Nicholas probably would've died for his faith in Jesus, but the emperor died first."

Hannah skipped into the next room, and I must admit that I felt pretty proud of myself. Not only had I answered Hannah's question, but I had also provided a lesson in history and generosity. What amazing wisdom God had provided to my daughter through me!

Or so I thought until the next afternoon.

In case you didn't know already, first-graders can really be blabbermouths sometimes. Once they learn something new, they feel the need to tell everyone, even if not everyone really needs to know.

Which explains why, on the next day, several of Hannah's classmates ran crying to their teachers because Hannah's daddy—who knew everything about these sorts of things, according to Hannah—had informed Hannah that Santa Claus had been dead for a long time.

Not only that, but an evil king had tortured him in a dungeon.

Let me tell you, there are certain children in this world who get way too worked up when it comes to the death of Santa Claus. And when children get worked up, parents and teachers get worked up too. Somehow I had lived several years under the peaceful delusion that once you graduate from high school, you can't get in trouble at school anymore. I was wrong about that.

Hannah had told the truth, but the truth hurt worse than she ever imagined it would.

It was somewhat that way when the results of my research into family discipleship came back. For so long, I had seen parents as the problem. I thought most parents were simply denying their responsibility for their children's spiritual development, but I had located the problem in the wrong place. The greater problem was the church's failure to acknowledge or equip parents as primary disciple-makers in their children's lives.

This truth hurt worse than I thought it would, because it forced me to take a painful look at my own history as a youth minister and to consider how little I had done to equip parents. Parents in my congregation probably sensed their responsibility as clearly as those in my research sample. They too were under-equipped and overly busy but I never tried to equip them. And I compounded their busyness by adding more activities for their children. Simply put, my programs and methods had been part of the problem. On top of this, especially in my early years as a youth minister, I gave parents the impression that I didn't need their input. My volunteers and I had everything under control—or so I wanted parents to think.

When all the data was brought together, lack of time, lack of training, or both factors together accounted for 90 percent of the parents who had disengaged from their children's spiritual development. (For the purposes of this statistic, I defined disengaged as a failure to engage consistently in any form of prayer or Bible study with children.) Ten percent of these disengaged parents admitted that their churches had equipped them to disciple their children but that their families weren't making the time. Almost three out of ten suggested that they had the time to engage spiritually with their children but that their church had provided no guidance. A little more than half stated that both factors were descriptive of their families: They were too busy *and* their church had provided no consistent equipping or encouragement.

As far as I can tell, that's the truth about where we are. It may hurt a bit but, like the death of St. Nicholas, the truth is no less true simply because it makes us wince.

Family Survey Factors in Parental Disengagement from Family Discipleship	
	Percentage of Parents
Lack of training only	28 percent
Lack of time only	10 percent
Both lack of training and lack of time	52 percent
Neither lack of training nor lack of time	10 percent

WHAT PARENTS REALLY NEED: TELLING, TRAINING, AND TIME

Let's pull together in a few paragraphs what we've learned thus far in this book about families in our churches: Most parents are not consistently engaged in any intentional processes of discipleship with their children. Parents typically value their children as gifts from God and seek to change their children's less desirable behaviors but they are making few intentional investments in their children's lives in light of redemption and eternity.

This lack of engagement is not, however, because parents are somehow unaware of their divinely designated responsibility. In fact, parents in churches overwhelmingly affirm that they are the people primarily responsible for their children's spiritual growth.

Why, then, are most of these same parents failing to engage in any intentional and consistent spiritual training in their households? A significant minority of moms and dads have traded spiritual growth for a schedule that's focused on success in sports and schooling. These parents need to experience gospel-centered transformation in their priorities. In many churches, this transformation is unlikely to happen in parents' lives until the calendars of ministry leaders are uncluttered to show them a better way.

The majority of parents have abdicated their role for a far different reason: In the words of the church member who waited for me after the worship service, "No one ever told me how." When it comes to planning for spiritual growth in their children's lives, parents have received little or no guidance from their churches. Most have never even been asked how their churches might help them to disciple their children. Parents in this category need to be acknowledged and equipped to guide their children's spiritual growth.

In the simplest possible terms, parents must be told, trained, and make the time.

But how can the church help? How can church leaders acknowledge and equip parents to pursue their God-ordained role?

What needs to happen so that, instead of usurping a role that God has placed at the feet of parents, church ministries guide parents to engage consistently and intentionally in the growth of their children's souls?

How can ministries clear their calendars to create the time that parents need to disciple their children?

That's what the last bit of this book is all about.

FAMILY MINISTRY FOR THE LONG-TERM

"Is anybody out there actually doing what we've described?"

That's the question that I found myself asking when I first developed the concepts that have now coalesced in this book. My colleague Randy Stinson and I had envisioned a distinct approach to family ministry—one that was theologically grounded and yet practical; something that provided churches with a clear vision for equipping parents without becoming simply another program.

Although we agreed that age-organized programs have often cut off parents from their disciple-making role in their children's lives, we still saw some value in focused ministries for children, youth, singles, senior adults, and other age-groupings. At the same time, we knew that it is not enough simply to add a few family friendly activities to what churches are already doing. Activity-driven approaches, while perhaps a positive first step for many churches, will never be sufficient to equip parents to disciple their children. Parents need training, to make the time, and to be told that God has called them to play a crucial role in their children's spiritual development. This will require churches to rethink and rework their age-organized ministries in radical ways.

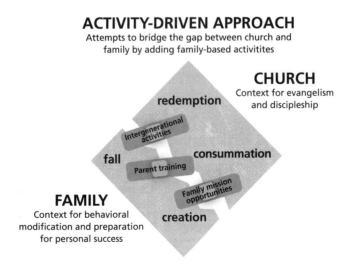

ACTIVITY-DRIVEN APPROACH
Attempts to bridge the gap between church and family by adding family-based activitites

CHURCH
Context for evangelism and discipleship

redemption

Intergenerational activities

fall

consummation

Parent training

FAMILY
Context for behavioral modification and preparation for personal success

Family mission opportunities

creation

And so, Randy and I developed the theological foundations for the approach that I eventually dubbed the "family-equipping ministry model."

Early in the process, I wondered at least a few times whether anyone would be willing to do what we had envisioned. I had been engaged in some of these practices during the last few years that I had served as a pastor, but I felt fairly certain that I was alone in what I was doing.

I soon discovered that I had not been alone after all.

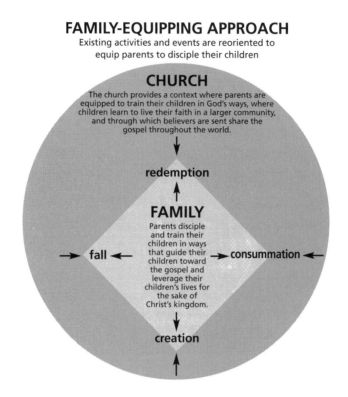

FAMILY-EQUIPPING APPROACH
Existing activities and events are reoriented to
equip parents to disciple their children

CHURCH
The church provides a context where parents are
equipped to train their children in God's ways, where
children learn to live their faith in a larger community,
and through which believers are sent share the
gospel throughout the world.

redemption

FAMILY
Parents disciple
and train their
children in ways
that guide their
children toward
the gospel and
leverage their
children's lives for
the sake of
Christ's kingdom.

fall

consummation

creation

Randy began to visit churches throughout the United States and soon gathered an informal coalition of ministry leaders who were already doing in practice precisely what we had sketched out in theory. Many of these leaders had never even met, yet they were pursuing models of ministry that were similar in significant ways. Steve Wright in North Carolina called it "co-championing church and home." Jay Strother in Tennessee and Brian Haynes in Texas were referring to parents as "primary faith trainers." Brian had also implemented a process for a lifelong partnership between church and home that he called "legacy milestones," and so on. As the number of participants in the discussion increased, we sharpened, corrected, and learned from one another.

CORE VALUES OF A FAMILY-EQUIPPING MINISTRY

Coordination around a Strategic Question

The precise wording may differ, but most family-equipping ministries make plans with a very specific strategic question in mind. This question functions as a filter to reshape or eliminate activities that might work against equipping parents to disciple their children. For example, the ministry team might ask, "How will this event equip parents to view themselves as the primary disciple-makers in their children's lives?" or "How will we train, involve, or equip parents through this activity?" If the projected activity does not clearly call parents to engage in their children's spiritual development, the activity is shelved or reworked.

Parenting with an Eternal Goal

As part of equipping parents, a strong emphasis is placed on rethinking the purpose of parenthood. The purpose of parenting is not to raise happy and successful adults but to lovingly leverage children's lives to advance God's kingdom so that every tribe, nation, and people-group gains the opportunity to respond in faith to the rightful King of kings. Parents receive encouragement to rethink their priorities and family schedules with this purpose in mind.

Parenting with a Lifelong Plan

Family-equipping ministries develop milestones or rites of passage in the lives of children and youth. Each milestone is preceded by a period of intentional parental instruction. Parents and ministries then partner together to prepare students for these milestones and celebrate them with the entire community of faith. For students whose parents will not participate, the church provides families in faith for the purpose of including these students.

Appreciation for the Generations

While recognizing the value of some age-organized learning experiences, family-equipping ministries emphasize opportunities for intergenerational integration and appreciation, with a particular emphasis on helping younger people to learn from older believers.

Faith Training in the Home

Family-equipping ministries consistently and intentionally equip parents to engage in faith training in their households.

High Expectations for Christian Husbands and Fathers

Recognizing the responsibility of Christian husbands and fathers to set the spiritual direction in their households, family-equipping ministries provide resources and training for husbands and fathers to guide their families.

Active Compassion for Spiritual Orphans

Recognizing that Christian parents are not present in every household, family-equipping ministries develop comprehensive plans for mentoring and discipling students whose fathers or mothers are not believers, while simultaneously seeking the salvation and spiritual growth of those parents.

Perhaps most significantly, our coalition explored how ministries managed the transition to family-equipping effectively. What emerged from these dialogues was a coherent, field-tested ministry model with clear core values that could be transferred to almost any context. Soon, we found a multitude of ministers who wanted to do family ministry but also needed guidance to metamorphose their ministries. That led to consultations that have spanned the globe and to churches around the world that have taken steps toward family-equipping ministry.

FOUR TRANSITIONS TO MOVE YOUR MINISTRY TOWARD FAMILY-EQUIPPING

1. From doing to being: Family-equipping ministry is not a program or a curriculum that a church does; it is an expression of our identity in Jesus Christ which calls Christian parents to raise children not only as their children but also as potential or actual brothers and sisters in Jesus Christ.
2. From expecting to equipping: Instead of expecting that parents already know how to disciple their children, family-equipping ministries reshape existing activities to equip parents with the skills they need to become primary disciple-makers in their children's lives.
3. From assuming to acknowledging: Instead of assuming that parents already know what to do to become primary disciple-makers in their children's lives, family-equipping ministries intentionally overcommunicate, taking every opportunity to acknowledge parents' divinely designated role.
4. From segmentation to synchronization: Recognizing that parents are the persons that God has positioned as primary disciple-makers in their children's lives, family-equipping ministries reshape activities for children and youth until every activity trains, involves, or equips families to practice at home what is learned in the larger community of faith. The church, instead of replacing what happens at home, supplements and reinforces the faith training that occurs in Christian households.

I must warn you, though: This transition is not quick or easy; it can be messy and will take time. If you plan to guide a ministry in the direction of family-equipping, don't think in terms of weeks or months; think years. Think about gradually changing the culture of a ministry so that parental discipleship of children becomes the norm instead of the exception. Parents need telling; parents need training; and parents must make the time—but none of these needs can be fulfilled instantly.

The foundations that I have presented thus far in this book will take months, at the very least, to put into play. The four transitions on the previous page could take years. Do what you do "with great patience and careful instruction" (2 Tim. 4:2). Seek transformation not through power plays or personality campaigns but through the systematic teaching of God's Word. Your goal is not to muster followers for your program but to equip servant-leaders who will in turn equip others to see every child as a potential or actual brother or sister in Christ.

"Re-culturing" of this sort requires deliberate and incremental course corrections that unfold over months and years. Moving too rapidly without first developing vital foundations and relationships can quickly kill the very changes that most need to be made. When it comes to re-culturing a ministry, the early bird may get the worm, but it's often the second mouse that gets the cheese. Don't look for the quickest route; look for the pathway that will lead to lasting change.

WHAT TO LOOK FOR IN THE FIELD

Guidance that parents need

THE KEY CONSIDERATION

In what ways are we presently guiding parents to become primary disciple-makers in their children's lives?

HOW TO FIND WHAT YOU'RE LOOKING FOR

Worksheet D: What Message Are We Sending?

WHAT TO DO

Gather your family ministry team. Using Worksheet D: What Message Are We Sending? look at the events, activities, and teaching that parents and participants in your ministry might have experienced in the past month.

Honestly assess whether your ministry is acknowledging or guiding parents to be primary disciple-makers in their children's lives. Based on what you know now, revisit and revise the tentative mission statement you developed earlier.

WHEN TO DO IT

At least one month before you plan to begin the transition to family ministry

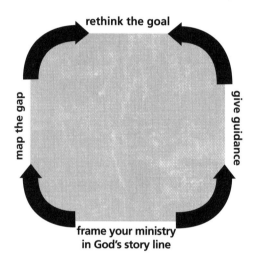

rethink the goal

map the gap

give guidance

**frame your ministry
in God's story line**

THINK ABOUT IT TOGETHER

Work through these activities with the family ministry team to develop a shared vision for your congregation's family ministry.

1. Develop an in-depth study of Genesis 22:1–19; Hebrews 11:16–19; and Romans 8:32. Focus on God's call to Abraham to be willing to give up his hopes for his son for the sake of obedience to God's Word, as well as the willingness of God the Father to give his only Son in our place. Consider how parents can allow dreams for their children's personal

happiness, present popularity, or vocational success to become false gods in their lives. You may find helpful the introduction and first chapter of Tim Keller, *Counterfeit Gods: The Empty Promises of Money, Sex, and Power, and the Only Hope That Matters* (New York: Penguin, 2009).

2. Discuss the hopes and expectations that parents in your ministry have for their children. Are these hopes rooted in the false assumption that the purpose of parenting is to raise happy and vocationally successful adults? Or do these hopes arise from a gospel-centered longing to leverage children's lives for the sake of Christ and his kingdom?

3. Prayerfully consider what habits or practices in your ministry might contribute to parents' fixation on personal happiness and measurable success. Does your planning focus on how to make participants happy instead of aiming them toward gospel transformation? Do your assessments of events rely on visible successes and budget numbers or on whether Scripture was faithfully and understandably proclaimed?

4. What are your hopes for your children, whether present or future? If you do not have children, are you mentoring any? If so, what are your hopes for them? Are these hopes authentically God-centered? What have you done in the past week to see God-centered hopes realized in the lives of your children? Where have you become caught up in the idolatrous dreams of the culture?

5. "No one ever told me how to do anything like that before," the woman said when she finally glimpsed how her family might engage in faith training at home. Could members in your church make a similar statement? If so, what has kept your congregation from acknowledging or equipping parents as primary disciple-makers in their children's lives?

RESOURCES TO HELP YOU GIVE PARENTS
THE GUIDANCE THEY NEED

Hemphill, Ken and Richard Ross. *Parenting with Kingdom Purpose*. Nashville, Tenn.: B&H, 2005.

Rienow, Rob. *Visionary Parenting: Capture a God-Sized Vision for Your Family*. Nashville, Tenn.: Randall House, 2009.

Strother, Jay. "Making the Transition to Family-Equipping Ministry." In *Trained in the Fear of God*, edited by Randy Stinson and Timothy Paul Jones. Grand Rapids, Mich.: Kregel Academic, 2011.

Wilson, Rodney and Selma. *The Parent Adventure*. Nashville, Tenn.: B&H, 2009.

FOUNDATION 5
TRANSITION TO FAMILY-EQUIPPING

KILLING THE ONE-EARED
MICKEY MOUSE

"A one-eared Mickey Mouse."

That's how one youth minister in the late 1980s depicted the relationship between his ministry and the rest of the congregation. In his picturesque analogy, the head of the cartoon mouse represented the church as a whole, and the ear represented youth ministry.[1]

The youth minister's point was simply this: Like the ear of the renowned mouse on Walt Disney's drawing board, his ministry was barely connected to the rest of the body. Although the student ministry and the larger congregation were technically linked, the two operated on separate tracks, with each one pursuing its own purposes and passions.

His church wasn't alone when he wrote those words.

It still isn't.

Conceived in the late nineteenth century and professionalized at the height of the baby boom, the one-eared Mickey Mouse turned out to be an attractive option for churches in the twentieth century. By segmenting the generations, churches didn't have to directly deal with the emerging generation gap. Youth had their own activities for themselves and their peers, separate from other generations. Though initially intended to attract unsaved teens, these activities quickly became aimed at retaining teenagers in the church until they became adults and rejoined the rest of the body.

During the second half of the twentieth century, the one-eared Mickey Mouse grew so popular that, in an overwhelming majority of midsized and larger churches, it became the presumed paradigm not only for youth but also for preschoolers, children, singles, and senior adults too. A one-eared mouse morphed into a multi-eared mutant.

And so, during a typical month in many churches, the preschool director plans a pleasant environment where toddlers can safely play and learn during the worship celebration. The children's minister recruits volunteers for an array of Bible memory programs and junior choirs. The youth learn Scripture and theology at camps or retreats and youth group meetings. The singles and senior adults each have their own rosters of resources and events, parents have small group meetings, men have a monthly breakfast, and women have their missions meetings.

And what's wrong with all these activities? Absolutely nothing, in and of themselves.

Nothing is wrong with camps, retreats, or gatherings of believers to study Scripture. The problem is that these activities have become so radically segmented that different generations rarely interact with one another. Even worse, parents are neither acknowledged nor equipped as primary disciplemakers in their children's lives. Parents remain untold and untrained when it comes to discipling their children—and, with so many activities on the roster, many parents don't have enough time to disciple their children even if they know how.

This is church as the twenty-first century knows it, as the twentieth century refined it, and as the nineteenth century created it. Some persons have referred to this arrangement as a "silo approach," where hired hands provide spiritual sustenance for each age-grouping by means of separate organizational structures. The academic phrase for such a structure is "segmented-programmatic." But I prefer another youth leader's far more memorable image. He described the segmented-programmatic church as something like "an octopus without a brain, a collection of arms acting independently with no central processing unit coordinating their actions."[2] In such congregations, family ministry—if it exists at all—is simply one more arm on the stereotypical cephalopod, flailing after time slots on the calendar and a line item in the budget.

THE ONE-EARED MICKEY MOUSE AND OCTOPUS WITHOUT A BRAIN

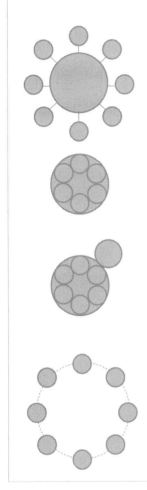

Societies (late 1800s and early 1900s)
In the era of societies, one congregation might have Sunday schools for each age-group, mission societies, temperance leagues, young people's prayer meetings, literary societies, a Young People's Association—all in addition to a Christian Endeavor society for youth and perhaps one or more Endeavor societies for children and adults. Each society ran parallel to others while the goals and curricula of each group remained unrelated. The church's connection to the societies was often loose and informal.

Efficiency (early to mid-1900s)
The societies of the previous generation became the church-based programs of this generation. In this initial movement toward the segmented-programmatic church, programs were streamlined, combined, and centralized.

Separation (mid-1900s)
Faced with the emerging generation gap between adolescents and their parents, parachurch organizations attempted to reach youth directly, bypassing parents and communities of faith. Churches tried to replicate the "youth groups" that Young Life and Youth for Christ had developed, even hiring youth ministers with the goal of attracting and retaining youth in these groups. The result was the "one-eared Mickey Mouse"—churches with youth ministries that were barely attached to the rest of the body.

Segmentation (late 1900s to present)
A separate ministry with separate activities and a separate track for youth seemed attractive not only for youth but also for other age-groups. Singles, children, senior adults, and other groups soon developed their own segmented programs with their own worship experiences, activities, and goals until no central point of reference remained in many churches. The identity of the church became the sum total of its separate programs. The result was the "octopus without a brain."

BRINGING THE GENERATIONS BACK TOGETHER

Today, the octopus without a brain remains the predominant model of ministry in many churches. But not everyone sees the octopus as the most faithful way of organizing the church of Jesus Christ. Even at the end of the twentieth century, a grassroots movement of pastors and youth ministry professionals had begun to point out some serious problems with mutant mice and mindless cephalopods.

The segmented-programmatic church had seemed quite successful when it came to providing lots of age-organized activities, but this bulk of programs came at a cost. Age segmentation became so systematic that the organizational structures in many churches complicated or even eliminated the possibility of different generations interacting with one another. Churches were providing parents with little encouragement and no equipping when it came to their children's spiritual development. After all, why equip parents to do something that the church was already paying youth and children's ministers to do?

SKETCH THE SITUATION

In the space below, draw an octopus arm for each ministry in your church. Label each arm. Now honestly consider: What is the organizational brain at the center in your congregation? Yes, I know, Jesus, the Bible, and the glory of God are supposed to be at the center, but what is the central decisive person or ideal that shapes the organization of each ministry in the congregation? If there is no central organizing factor, leave the center blank.

In many churches, no central organizing system exists or the central organizing system is simply the word of a strong leader or a vague dream for the church's future, neither of which can sustain long-term coordination of the church's ministries.

The aim of family ministry is not to eliminate every arm. Some sort of organizational arms will exist in any congregation of believers and these diverse organizational segments are not necessarily wrong. Spirit-guided coordination of diverse members of the body is a thoroughly biblical concept (1 Cor. 12:12–27). The first Christians gathered not only in large groups but also "house to house" (Acts 2:46 NASB), implying a pattern of organizing in smaller groups. Family ministry synchronizes the church's groups around a clear strategic question and coordinates ministries in ways that equip parents as primary faith trainers in their children's lives.

All of this segmentation might be acceptable if it weren't for a single critical snag: Social or generational similarities are not what define Christian fellowship. The people of God are shaped and defined by Jesus Christ himself, who unites individuals that the world would never dream of bringing together—but not by clustering them in categories of age or special interest or musical preference. Oneness based on such fleeting demographic categories is the same sort of pseudo-unity that the world already offers in the form of tightly niched television programs and marketing campaigns.

Jesus Christ has bonded believers together once and for all by breaking down the barriers between them on the basis of his own blood (Eph. 2:14–15). Part of the scandal of the cross is the fact that those who rub shoulders in the shadow of the cross are precisely the people that would never naturally mingle with one another—brothers and sisters from different people groups and nations and generations. That's why the Holy Spirit of God, speaking through the words of Scripture, specifically calls for close intergenerational connections among God's people (Titus 2:1–5) as well as discipleship that flows from the fathers of one generation to the children of the next (Eph. 6:4; Col. 3:21; see also Mal. 4:6; Luke 1:17). These are not issues of preference or convenience. They are issues of faithfulness to God's design for his church and they are rooted in the gospel itself.

> Suppose that a faithful senior citizen who's been a long time member of your congregation dies. How many youth—other than those who might be related to that individual—would be affected by this person's passing? How many children? If very few youth or children are sufficiently connected to senior adults to be saddened when one of them passes away, what does this say about generational segmentation in your church? Do such divisions reflect God's design for his people?

And so, convinced that neither systematic age segmentation nor professionalized discipleship of children rightly reflects God's design for his people, a rising tide of church leaders began asking, "How do we bring the generations back together?" Or to put it in slightly more graphic terms, "How do we kill an octopus that seems to have lost its mind?" As the twentieth century faded into the twenty-first, three distinct models of family ministry emerged in evangelical churches. Each model endeavors to drown the octopus in a slightly different way.

THREE WAYS TO KILL AN OCTOPUS

The three primary models of family ministry that have emerged over the past couple of decades are *family-based, family-integrated,* and *family-equipping.* According to people who study organizational systems and models for a living, a model must meet a handful of specific characteristics to qualify as a model. To understand what's intended in this book by a ministry model, let's first take a quick look at the general criteria for a model:

A MODEL COMES FROM SOMETHING THAT ALREADY EXISTS
A model is based on an existing object or system. If there's no existing object or system, it's a theory or an idea not a model. Each family ministry model that I'm presenting here has actually been implemented in local churches.

A MODEL CAN BE SUMMARIZED IN AN ABBREVIATED FORM
A model includes only relevant properties from the original object or system. If it included everything from the original, it wouldn't be a model. It would be a copy. Within each of the three family ministry models, certain properties remain constant from one context to another, suggesting a system of relevant characteristics in each model that makes that model distinct.

A MODEL IS CAPABLE OF BEING PRACTICALLY APPLIED IN OTHER CONTEXTS
A model is transferable and applicable in situations beyond the original context. If it doesn't work outside the original context, it's not a model; it's a system that's embedded in and dependent on its original environment. Each of the three primary family ministry models has been implemented in some form in a variety of social contexts.[3]

So how does each family ministry model work in real life? Let's consider each one to see.

1. The family-based ministry model: Mark DeVries pioneered the family-based ministry model in the 1990s through his groundbreaking

book *Family-Based Youth Ministry.* Family-based ministries support families by adding or expanding events to provide different age-groups with excuses to interact together. The result is a smorgasbord of activities to connect youth and children with their parents and other persons from a variety of generations. In a family-based church calendar, you're likely to find everything from a father-daughter banquet to a community outreach event where older and younger folk serve together; from a mother-son date night to a family mission trip or family camp, in addition to youth mission trips and youth camps.

2. The family-integrated ministry model: The family-integrated model takes a very different approach to tackling over-segmented church programs. Instead of adding activities or combining events that are already happening, family-integrated ministries remove every hint of generational segmentation. Finding insufficient biblical foundations for age-organized ministries, proponents of family integration make every activity and event intergenerational. That's right: no nurseries, no age-graded classes, no youth groups, and no senior adult outings. The entire congregation is restructured to require parents, and particularly fathers, to disciple their households. The family-integrated ministry model has been around for many years, but one of the most popular recent presentations has been in the book from Voddie Baucham entitled *Family-Driven Faith.*

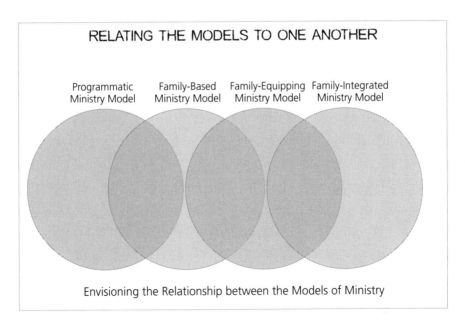

RELATING THE MODELS TO ONE ANOTHER

Programmatic Ministry Model • Family-Based Ministry Model • Family-Equipping Ministry Model • Family-Integrated Ministry Model

Envisioning the Relationship between the Models of Ministry

3. The family-equipping ministry model: Family-equipping represents a third possibility for family ministry. This model steers a distinct course between the previous two. In its simplest definition, family-equipping ministry simply means coordinating every aspect of your present ministry so that parents are acknowledged, equipped, and held accountable as primary disciple-makers in their children's lives. Family-equipping ministry is all about reorienting activities that are already happening so that parents are equipped to become primary disciple-makers in their children's lives. The focus of family-equipping is not an increase in family activities but a deepening of gospel identity. Once family-equipping takes root and permeates every aspect of your ministry, you will likely find yourself combining or cutting some activities, doing less so that parents have time to do more.

Family-equipping leaders recognize with proponents of family-integrated ministry that age-organized programs, as they are presently practiced, have failed to empower parents as primary disciple-makers in their children's lives. At the same time, the family-equipping model (a bit more like family-based at this point) still sees a valid place for age-organized ministries. God places people in distinct roles within the church (Eph. 4:11–16). As such, it seems that some ministers could be gifted to relate primarily to families with children in a particular stage of life just as other ministers might be particularly skilled in worship leadership or administration. And so, in family-equipping ministries, age-focused ministers and volunteers remain in place, but they find themselves playing very different roles than ever before.

BEGINNING BENEATH THE SURFACE

I need to make a candid confession at this point—one that you may already have guessed: I am biased when it comes to family-equipping. I am convinced that, for most church ministries, the family-equipping ministry model is the best way to leave behind the proverbial octopus.

At the same time, I don't see family-based or family-integrated ministries as foes or even as competitors. All three ministry models share a common goal of partnering with parents so that they become primary disciple-makers in their children's lives. At least a few elements of each one tend to be woven throughout one or both of the others.

Models for Ministry to Families

	Segmented-Programmatic Ministry Model	Family-Based Ministry Model	Family-Equipping Ministry Model	Family-Integrated Ministry Model
What does this model look like in the local church?	Ministries are organized in separate "silos" with little consistent intergenerational interaction. Family ministry, if it exists, is simply one more program. The program may provide training, intervention, or activities for families. In scheduling programs, churches may deliberately seek to be sensitive to family's needs and schedules.	Programmatic structures remain unchanged, but each separate ministry plans and programs activities that intentionally draw generations together and invite parents to take part in the discipleship of their children and youth.	Although age-organized programs and events still exist, the ministry is completely restructured to draw generations together, equipping parents, championing their role as primary disciple-makers, and holding them accountable to fulfill this role.	The church eliminates age-segregated programs and events. All or nearly all programs and events are multi-generational, with a strong focus on parents' responsibility to use their household as a context for evangelizing and discipling not only their own families but also others, inside and outside the faith community.
What other approaches might be included in this ministry model?	Therapeutic-Counseling Family Ministry (Chap Clark) Church-Centered/Home-Supported Ministry (Ben Freudenburg) Family-Sensitive Ministry (Michelle Anthony)	Family-Friendly Youth Ministry; Family-Focused Youth Ministry (Dave Rahn) Family-Based Youth Ministry (Mark DeVries) Family-Friendly Ministry (Michelle Anthony)	Youth-Focused Family Ministry; Youth-Friendly Family Ministry (Dave Rahn) Home-Centered/Church-Supported Ministry (Ben Freudenburg) Co-Champion Model (Steve Wright) Family-Empowered Ministry (Michelle Anthony)	Family Discipleship Model (Alliance for Church and Family Reformation) Family-Centered Ministry (Michelle Anthony) Inclusive-Congregational Ministry (Malan Nel)

Family-based ministry adds more activities or merges current activities. Family-integrated ministry subtracts age-segregated activities. Family-equipping ministry multiplies the impact of what churches are already doing by transforming age-organized activities into partnerships that span the generations.

The transition strategies for these three models aren't exclusive of one another either. In fact, I've glimpsed a consistent pattern while consulting with different churches that were in transition toward different family ministry models. Perhaps because family-equipping steers a middle ground between the other two models, transitional strategies that work for moving toward family-equipping ministry are equally effective in shifting ministries toward family-based or family-integrated ministry. And so, regardless of the family ministry model that God has called you to pursue, the transitional strategies that have taken other ministries in the direction of family-equipping are likely to be helpful in your ministry too.

What I'm about to present in the remainder of this book has been developed from the collective wisdom of several leaders who made the shift from segmented-programmatic ministry to a comprehensive family-equipping model. I engaged with these leaders in what's known as a Delphi method study; that's simply a systematic way of finding consensus about how to proceed in a particular area. What I learned is that, even though their churches and ministries were very different, there were common elements that they saw as necessary to make the transition to family-equipping. What's more, there was a solid consensus when it came to certain perceptions and practices that ought to mark a family-equipping ministry.

A word of warning before we begin, though: These marks and transitional strategies will look slightly different in every church, and they are not the essence of family ministry. They are simply the outward expressions of the deep-rooted biblical truths in the chapters that have preceded this one. Gospel-centered family ministry has more to do with the unseen foundations than with the visible practices. If you attempt to implement these outward expressions without first rethinking the foundations, your family ministry will be one more short-lived program, structured on the shifting sands of human pragmatism.

Here's how my friend and fellow family-equipper Jay Strother illustrates the importance of the biblical foundations in family-equipping ministry:

Imagine an iceberg floating in the ocean. Two-thirds of the mass of the iceberg rests below the water, unseen from the surface. Now, imagine the structure of your ministry with families. That critical mass beneath the surface is the essential theological foundation that makes everything else possible. Above the surface of the water, it will be possible to see some distinctive practices of your particular ministry. These practices might even be what you notice first when you visit this ministry. But these outward marks are not the essence of the family ministry. They are the effects of far deeper perceptions and practices.

The essence of family ministry is the biblical foundation and renewed outlook that remain beneath the surface, unseen but supporting everything else. The outward practices are important, but they are not the primary point. That's why the first transition requires a shift in your ministry leadership from doing activities to embracing an identity.

> The earliest English usage of the term "family ministry" in a religious context seems to have been in *The Home Life, In the Light of Its Divine Idea* by James Baldwin Brown. What this author meant by family ministry was not the church's ministry to families but the family's ministry to the world. Family ministry described how families demonstrated the love of Jesus Christ to the poor, the fatherless, and the widow. In what ways might your church recover this aspect of family ministry?

FAMILY-EQUIPPING TRANSITION 1:
BE

"So what do we do first?" he asks. I notice dozens of heads in this gathering of ministry leaders nodding together in response to his question. That's what they're wondering too—and now, as always, it's my least favorite question to answer.

I have stood before thousands of pastors and students over the past few years, talking about family ministry, and the question of what to do first is the toughest question I face. The problem isn't that I lack an answer. What's difficult is that, in most cases, my answer isn't even close to what the questioner wants to hear.

What this person typically wants is a detailed organizational action plan. Do we add a family pastor first? Or do we shuffle the responsibilities among the staff we already have? Do we rename our gymnasium a "family life center"? Do you know of a good family camp? Should we switch our Sunday school curriculum? If so, when?

None of these considerations are wrong, but none of them are where family-equipping ministry begins. Family-equipping ministry isn't primarily an organizational activity. It flows out of who you are, beginning with the ministry leaders.

Which is why I answer his query with a question of my own: "What have you done in the past seven days to disciple your family?"

I then add, "Your church's family-equipping ministry doesn't begin in an administrative meeting or a business session or the pastor's personal planning retreat. Family-equipping begins in the homes of the leaders in your ministry—in the pastor's den, at the deacon's dining room table, in the youth minister's car. You can't lead a family ministry with any degree of integrity unless you become a family minister in your own household. *Be* before you *do*."

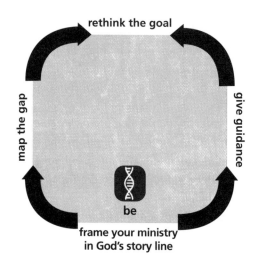

LIKE THE PLUMBER WHO WON'T FIX HIS OWN FAUCET

One pattern that became clear as I surveyed churches was that it's not enough to change the church organization. Family-equipping ministry requires ministry leaders to come to terms with their own failures and struggles when it comes to family discipleship. This sort of transparency and honesty doesn't come easily, but it is an essential first step toward full-fledged family-equipping.

The apostle Paul spent a single extended sentence (six verses in most English translations) in one of his letters summing up the qualifications for a pastor (1 Tim. 3:2–7). Two of those six verses spell out specific expectations related to the leader's household (1 Tim. 3:4–5).

Think about the structure of this passage for a moment: Paul plowed through administrative and teaching skills in only a few words. But he spent one-third of this text on the single issue of a pastor's home life. Compare Paul's words with the pastoral job descriptions in denominational magazines or on websites for ministers who are looking to change churches. Compared to these contemporary job descriptions, Paul's listing seems ridiculously imbalanced, too little text focused on specific skills and too much ink spilled over a pastor's integrity in the family.

Why such a focus on the minister's family? The apostle's Spirit-inspired response is that, if leaders can't guide their own households, how can they possibly lead God's household? (1 Tim. 3:5).

Think of it this way: Would you trust a plumber whose kitchen has a perpetually leaky faucet? What about a mechanic whose oil never gets changed or whose check engine light never gets checked?

Ministers who try to lead the ministries of the church without discipling their own families are in precisely the same predicament as the plumber who won't fix his dripping faucet or the mechanic whose dipstick is dry.

This is not to say that Christian leaders should turn their children or spouses into perfectly ordered pawns in their own personal publicity campaigns. Even in the homes of the church's best leaders, diapers still get full, gas tanks still get empty, and some months still outlast the balance in the checking account. Words are spoken that should never even have been thought, and children make choices that are far from cherubic. And yet, even with these challenges and more, every Christian household can become a context where the gospel is consistently rehearsed and where parents and children alike confess their failures to one another and learn to turn to Jesus. Particularly in a pastor's family, parents must be deeply involved in discipling their children toward godliness.

But there's more to this text than a calling for pastors to manage their households. Paul's focus in this list of pastoral qualifications also implies a principle that reaches far beyond the people that happen to be ordained. The principle is simply this: What you accomplish for God beyond your home will typically never be greater than what you practice with God within your home.

That's why family ministry cannot merely be a series of activities that a congregation does. It must flow from who the leaders and volunteers are with their families, day by day. As this identity takes root in their homes, they become better able to guide their ministries in the direction of equipping families.

Does this mean, then, that the focus of ministry leaders should be primarily on their own homes and the homes of church families? Yes and no. Yes, ministry leaders should place a priority on rehearsing the gospel in their own households, but whenever the gospel is authentically rehearsed in our homes, we are compelled to share it not only with those in our own households, but also with those who are far from where we are. It's what I call the Grover Principle.

THE GROVER PRINCIPLE

"Sunny days, sweepin' the clouds away. On my way to where the air is sweet. Can you tell me how to get, how to get to . . . ?" If that couplet strikes a chord in your memories of childhood, you were probably an avid viewer of the American PBS program known as *Sesame Street.* Bert and Ernie, Big Bird and Snuffleupagus, Gordon and Susan and Mr. Hooper—all of them were recurring characters in my life as a preschooler. One of my favorite characters was a furry blue monster known as Grover.

What I remember most clearly about Grover is a skit you may recall too. Grover began by running to the camera, pressing his pink nose toward the lens, and announcing that he was "Neeeaaarr!" Then he hurried into the distance and declared that he was now "Faaaarrr!" Over and over, Grover rushed from one end of the set to the other, near and then far. The blue puppet didn't settle for near, and he didn't stay far. He constantly alternated between the two.

That's how family-equipping ministry has to work too—and it must begin in the homes of ministry leaders.

It's not just about reaching those that are near, and it's not all about reaching those that are far. It's about both. Family-equipping begins with those that are near, our own families and the families in our churches, but then it moves immediately to those who are far. A passion to reach those who are far is good, but that passion does not give us permission to abandon or ignore those who are near.

That's what I mean by the Grover Principle.

For some ministry leaders, it's tempting to focus their ministries only on those who are near, on the church families who need to develop discipleship practices in their homes. Families in these churches do tend to develop holy habits, but such congregations may lack a passion for seeing the gospel take root in people whose lives might be messy.

Other leaders center on those who are far, designing their programs to bypass parents and reach children whose families are fractured and fragmented. The problem is this focus on reaching children directly can become so thoroughgoing that the church never explicitly expects any parents—even Christian parents—to disciple their children.

Family-equipping ministry recognizes that the gospel compels God's people to view every person as a potential or actual brother or sister in Christ. This passion begins with those who are near and then moves to those who are far, but the ministry with those who are far remains possible only because we continue to equip those who are near. Family-equipping ministry is about near and far.

> "Why aren't churches equipping parents to disciple their children? Because many pastors are struggling to lead their own homes spiritually. They are bogged down by administrative 'ministry.' They don't teach or preach on this because they themselves aren't doing it."
> —Jenny Rimsza Clark

Of course, none of this originated with the hyperactive blue puppet who lives on Sesame Street. The apostle Peter put it this way during the Feast of Pentecost: "This promise is for you and your children and for all who are far off" (Acts 2:39). Do you see the principle at work? The promise of the gospel is for those who are near, but this nearness compels us to share the Word with those who are far, so that the gospel becomes near to them as well.

WHY MINISTRY TO THOSE WHO ARE NEAR ISN'T ENOUGH

What does all of this have to do with moving family ministry from a flurry of activities to a process that flows out of our identities as ministry leaders? Whenever ministry leaders become passionate about family ministry (which is good!), it's easy to allow family ministry to become our identity or the identity that drives our ministry (and that's not so good). Then we begin to focus our ministries only on our own families and the families that are near.

But our families must never become our identity or the identity that drives our ministries. If you are a believer in Jesus Christ, he is your identity. "Your life is now hidden with Christ in God," and "Christ . . . is your life" (Col. 3:3–4). His gospel has set an ax to the root of any pretense that we are who we are because of our families (Matt. 3:9–10). To position anything other than this gospel as the focus of your ministry is to lapse into idolatry.

And what's the result of such an idolatrous misfocus? If the families who are near become the centerpiece of your ministry, what about the child for whom *family* implies a step-grandfather who has violated her until she flinches at the touch of any man? What about the youth whose mother has been absent since he was a toddler and who forges his father's signature on permission slips because his father isn't sufficiently sober to form a coherent sentence, let alone a signature? What about the institutionalized children in Romania and Russia and Ukraine who have never known a mother or father? Or the infants in Africa rendered fatherless by AIDS? And what of the thousands of children who wait in foster care systems around the world? How about the children a few blocks from your church building whose mothers or fathers are unbelievers? Where will these children fit in a ministry that focuses only on families who are near? If equipping families becomes the central battle cry of your ministry, who will recognize them as potential or actual brothers and sisters in Christ?

When the families that are near become the centerpiece of our ministries, we tend to lose sight of the plight of the orphan. The ravages of sin have filled this world with orphans—physical orphans whose parents have abandoned them, relational orphans whose fathers and mothers are too busy to hear their children's cries, and spiritual orphans whose parents have never embraced God's grace. The entire cosmos groans beneath this awful burden of broken families, fatherless children, and spiritual orphans. Yet the healing that the cosmos craves comes not through the development of healthy families but through the revealing of Jesus Christ in his glory, with a new family formed by the adoption of a host of blood-redeemed brothers and sisters (Rom. 8:16–23).

If the equipping of families becomes the identity that drives a ministry, the focus of the ministry will tend to begin and end with the development of healthy families. Yet earthly families are a means in God's plan, never a goal. God's work of redemption does not begin or end with families, healthy or otherwise. God's plan finds its genesis and fulfillment in Jesus Christ (Rev. 22:13; see also Col. 1:16–20; Heb. 12:2).

To bypass the orphan in favor of a focus on whole and healthy families is to neglect a heartbeat that has long marked the rhythms of God's redemptive plan (Ex. 22:22; Isa. 1:17; James 1:27). There are, after all, no natural-born children of God among us; there are only ex-orphans who have been brought into God's family through divine adoption (Rom. 8:15; 9:4; Gal. 4:5). From the instant Eve took her first taste of forbidden fruit, we have all been turned into orphans, abandoned by a deadbeat dad of the most devilish sort (John 8:41–44; 14:18).

There is, however, good news for those who sense their orphaned status: The power of the curse has been shattered because the only Son of God chose to be forsaken by his Father in our place (Mark 15:34). Through faith in him, we who were orphans become beloved children of God (John 11:51–52; 14:18; Gal. 3:26; 1 John 3:1). This was part of the plan long before God slipped into human history. Even in the Old Testament, God declared himself the father of the fatherless (Deut. 10:18; Ps. 27:10; 68:5; 146:9), pointing forward to the time when he would form a new family from every tribe and nation on the earth (Eph. 1:5; Rev. 5:9).

WHY GOING FAR REQUIRES US FIRST TO GO NEAR

Family ministry is not a series of activities. Family-equipping ministry in particular flows out of an identity that begins in the homes of ministry leaders. But this doesn't mean that equipping families should become the identity that drives our ministry. Jesus alone is our identity, and his gospel is our story. Anything more or less is idolatry.

This gospel-centered identity calls us to see every person as an orphan because of humanity's fall and as a potential brother or sister because of Christ's redemption. That is, at least in part, why Jesus blessed children indiscriminately and called his people to care for "the least of these." That's why Jesus called for outcasts to be invited to a banquet where they knew they didn't belong (Matt. 19:13–15; 25:31–46; Luke 14:12–24). Jesus saw every person's deepest need in the shadow of the fall and every person's grandest possibility in the light of the gospel. The essence of family-equipping ministry is the implementation of this gospel-centered identity first in our homes and then beyond our homes. The gospel is to be rehearsed in our homes and reinforced in our churches so that it can be revealed with integrity to the world.

Particularly for the ministry leader, the home is a divinely designed context for rehearsing the gospel. The Christian household is, in the words of Martin Luther, "a school for character."[1] But this school, like every other, school, is a temporary training ground, not the final goal. Because the home is not the final goal, family ministry remains incomplete until it results in the proclamation of the gospel beyond our families. Family ministry that never reaches beyond our households is like a regimen of spring training that never results in a real baseball game.

The problem for a significant proportion of pastors and ministry leaders is that they see their churches, and even their communities, in light of people's need for the gospel, but they fail to see their own families from this same perspective. They see the needs of those who are far, but they don't see the same needs in those who are nearest to them.

The student minister spends six months mapping out every detail of a weeklong youth camp. The volunteer in middle school ministry meets early every Monday morning to pray with a half dozen sixth graders about their week at school. The pastor is present at every community outreach event, and everyone praises his clear vision for the church's future. Yet the student minister can't seem to carve out a half hour each week to talk with his family about living in light of the gospel. The middle school prayer leader hasn't prayed with her husband in more than a decade. And, outside of keeping the children in church and hoping none of them does anything that causes a public scandal, neither the pastor nor the pastor's spouse has any clear vision for his children's spiritual formation.

In most cases, the root of these patterns is not deliberate rebellion against God. It is a misplaced perspective that fails to see the home as the ministry leader's first context for ministry. As a result, ministry leaders try to do ministry in their churches and communities without first becoming ministers in their own households.

REAL-LIFE IDEAS FOR MOVING FROM DOING TO BEING

The point of these ideas is not to provide a step-by-step guide to making the shift from doing to being. The point is to spark your thinking by providing you with examples of real-life practices that other ministries have used effectively.

Don't Wait for the Movie

Ministry teams frequently read and discuss books together—typically books about theology, leadership, or administration. At least once or twice each year, read and discuss a book together that challenges ministry leaders to become disciple-makers in their own households. Here are some suggested resources that have helped other ministry teams: Jim and Jerolyn Bogear, *Faith Legacy: Six Values to Shape Your Child's Journey* (Indianapolis, Ind.: Wesleyan Publishing House, 2009); William Farley, *Gospel-Powered Parenting: How the Gospel Shapes and Transforms Parenting* (Phillipsburg, N.J.: P&R Publishing, 2009); Rob Rienow, *Visionary Parenting: Capture a God-Sized Vision for Your Family* (Nashville, Tenn.: Randall House, 2009); Kelli B. Trujillo, *Faith-Filled Moments: Helping Kids See God in Everyday Life* (Indianapolis, Ind.: Wesleyan Publishing House, 2009); Steve Wright with Chris Graves, *ApParent Privilege* (Raleigh, N.C.: InQuest Ministries, 2008); John Younts, *Everyday Talk: Talking Freely and Naturally about God with Your Children* (Wapwallopen, Penn.: Shepherd Press, 2005). *continued*

REAL-LIFE IDEAS FOR MOVING FROM DOING TO BEING *continued*

Ask the Right Questions

Ministry teams can also function as accountability groups. Develop questions for each meeting to hold one another accountable for discipling children. Such questions might include, "What have you done since our last meeting to disciple your family? How has the gospel transformed your parenting practices over the past month? In what specific, planned ways are you engaging with your spouse, children, or the children of some other parent as a disciple-maker in their lives?" Set some simple expectations for ministry leaders in the area of family discipleship; talk about these expectations at each meeting and hold one another accountable.

Talk About What's Working in Your Own Homes and What Isn't

Develop an atmosphere of openness and mutual accountability by talking together about how you began to disciple your children. Share stories of family discipleship with one another, and not only the triumphs! Be ready to say, "Here's great idea that worked well in my family!" but also be willing to admit, "I am struggling in this area of family discipleship. Is anyone else having difficulties here? How can we pray for one another? What resources or help could we provide for one another?" You are likely to discover that many of your ministry leaders have never engaged in any discipleship practices with their own children. If so, do not respond by with pride by pointing to your own accomplishments. Work alongside your brother or sister; help your fellow believer to develop these habits not because of a guilt-driven sense of obligation but as a free and joyous response to the gospel (Rom. 15:1–7; Gal. 5:25—6:10).

Share Your Stories with Your Children

Many ministry leaders have never even told their children how they became believers in Jesus Christ. If ministry leaders haven't shared their testimonies in their own living rooms, it's unlikely that they will be very effective when it comes to sharing the gospel with persons beyond their homes. At your ministry team meeting, ask ministry leaders to share their faith-journeys with their children before the next meeting. Talk at the next meeting about the children's questions and responses to these testimonies. Encourage leaders to build on this sharing time by beginning a weekly practice of devotions with their families where family members share other stories of faith with one another.

Write Letters to Your Children

At your ministry team meeting, ask ministry leaders to write letters to each of their children, expressing their hopes and desires for their children's futures. If leaders do not have children, have them write letters to their future children or to children that they are presently mentoring. Use this opportunity to talk about how even Christian parents tend to embrace the world's goals for their children, chasing earthly happiness and success instead of eternal purposes. Ask ministry

continued

REAL-LIFE IDEAS FOR MOVING FROM DOING TO BEING *continued*

leaders to share their letters with their children before the next meeting. If a ministry leader's children are too small to understand or if the ministry leader wrote the letter to future children, encourage the ministry leader to share the letter with his or her spouse or a close friend. At the next meeting, share your letters with one another. Discuss what you learned by writing and sharing these letters. Encourage ministry leaders to build on their sharing time with spouse or children by developing a weekly habit of discussing eternal goals for their child's life. See page 149 for an example of a letter written by a youth pastor to his unborn child.

Turn Your Ministry Leaders into Guinea Pigs

Develop a weekly devotional guide for families. Ask your ministry leaders to test the devotionals with their own families and provide feedback at team meetings. The goal is eventually to provide these devotionals to families in your church, but by testing them with your ministry leaders, you are developing discipleship habits in the homes of your leaders.

Check Your Calendars

It's possible that your ministry leaders are too busy (perhaps even with church activities) to disciple their own families. Take a critical look at your calendars. Give each other the freedom to say no to some activities so that you have sufficient time to engage spiritually with your families.

MAKING THE SHIFT FROM DOING TO BEING

So what will it take to shift your ministry leaders toward gospel-centered equipping of families? When I presented that question to ministers whose churches had effectively made the transition to family-equipping, one word rose repeatedly to the top of the list: *repentance*. A critical first step toward family-equipping occurred when ministry leaders admitted that they hadn't been actively engaged in growing their children's souls and began to shift the priorities in their households.

Of course, you can't cause this sort of repentance; only the Holy Spirit can do that. What you can do is create a safe context where ministry leaders can consider their roles in discipling their families and where the Spirit can work freely in their hearts.

You probably already have regular meetings with ministry leaders or key volunteers, so don't add any more meetings to your calendar! Take advantage of times that are already on the calendar to create an atmosphere of partnership and accountability when it comes to family discipleship. These meetings are likely to look very different from one context to another. If you're the children's ministry director in a small congregation, these meetings may mean pulling together a handful of fellow volunteers once a month at a local café. If you're the senior pastor in a suburban megachurch, staff members from several separate ministries will probably be present with you in the conference room. In some congregations, your key gatherings could be deacons' meetings; in others, it might be with the board of elders. If you've already gathered a family ministry team, you can continue to develop this team.

Regardless of who is present or where you meet, your goal is to work together to view your own families and the families around you in light of God's story line. Certain habits and practices will flow out of this gospel-centered perspective, but the practices themselves aren't the primary point. The point is inward transformation, which is likely to take time.

Over a period of several months, map out each meeting so that key leaders are equipped and held accountable to actively engage in discipling their children. This doesn't mean that family-equipping becomes the focus of every meeting. It simply means that every meeting includes mention and movement in that direction.

If you or some of your leaders are single, partner in a particular way with one or more parents on your team. Become personally involved in their children's lives, perhaps even helping them to lead family worship from time to time or joining with them in processes of family discipleship. If you're married but don't have children, develop habits of prayer and worship with your spouse, as well as looking for opportunities to partner with parents. Regardless of your status, become involved in turning homes into centers for spiritual formation!

And how will you know when your key leaders have moved from trying to do family ministry to being family ministers in their homes? Listen. Listen carefully. Listen for eagerness in ministry leaders' voices as they share what's going on in their households and with the children that they disciple. When new volunteers or staff members join your team, hear how existing team members explain the expectation for family-equipping in your ministry.

Notice as the gospel begins to set the rhythms in the homes of ministry leaders. Listen as the cry of the orphan becomes woven into the fabric of your discussions and drives you to live out the gospel near and far.

A LETTER WRITTEN BY A YOUTH PASTOR TO HIS PRE-BORN CHILD

My child, you and I have not yet met face to face, but I have seen your shape being formed, and I have heard your heart beat. I cannot wait to hold you in my arms, to comfort you, to pick you up when you fall down, and to pray over you while you sleep. I look forward to the day Jesus becomes as real to you as your mommy and me.

I pray that you would know Christ.

I pray that you would feel the love of your daddy and mommy.

I pray that you would run to me when thunder claps, when the lights go out, when the monsters growl under your bed, and when you skin your knee.

I pray that you would love serving Jesus.

I pray (if you're a boy) that you would grow into a godly man, and that you would marry a woman like your mommy. I pray you would cherish her, love her, and be a strong man for her.

I pray (if you're a girl) that you would find a man who loves you as much as your daddy does, in whose arms you feel safe, that you would love him like your mommy loves your daddy. I pray that you would be loving, gracious, kind, and his greatest encouragement and helper.

I pray that you would grow academically, have your mommy's singing voice, be more coordinated than your daddy, and find joy in all you do.

I pray that no matter how much you love Mommy and Daddy, you would love Jesus more and that you would find all your joy and peace in him.

I pray that when it comes time to let you go, that you would go wherever God takes you.

I pray that you will have more faith than I did.

I pray you would have a heart for the nations, that you would love people who live far away and that you would pray for them and share Jesus with them.

My child, I don't want the American dream for you. I don't even know what the American dream will look like by the time you read this. But I do know this: I don't want you to be happy with more stuff or bigger vacations or an easier life. I want you to know Christ, to make him known, and to be willing to go wherever he takes you, regardless of the cost.

I love you.

Daddy

—Scott Douglas

FAMILY-EQUIPPING TRANSITION 2A: EQUIP FAMILIES FOR FAITH TALKS

The year that we adopted our oldest daughter, she attended first grade at a nearby Montessori school. There, she had quite a few struggles when it came to interacting constructively with other children. When things didn't go her way in a play group, someone inevitably ended up hurt, and that someone was never her.

Not wanting to be sued by the school or to raise a child who ended up as the dictator of some hapless Third World country, I made a list for her of things that it is best not to do to other people. This list included the many activities that she had already tried—hitting, kicking, scratching, and the like—plus a few that she hadn't yet considered but probably soon would, such as detonating thermonuclear weaponry in the art room. Each morning, I went through the list with her and pointed out how God calls us to value every person as someone created in his image. Everything went quite smoothly for almost a week. Then, on Friday afternoon, I received a call from the school.

"Your daughter has something that she would like to discuss with you," the school administrator said. She handed the telephone to my child, and the first words that I heard were, "Daddy, you didn't say anything about twisting people's arms." And she was right. I hadn't included that action on my list, and that's how I learned the danger of making a list. Once you make a list, it's easy to conclude that everything you need to do appears on the list, or, in my daughter's case, everything you need not to do.

My daughter has long since left behind her proclivities toward personal violence, but my hesitancy to rely on lists remains. I have no desire to provide the impression that once you complete a specific series of steps, you've done everything that's necessary for your church's family ministry. The fact is, you might do everything on my list, and then discover that, in your ministry, something additional was absolutely necessary all along. As family-equipping pastor Brian Haynes says, cookie cutters are for cookies, not church ministries. The particulars of family-equipping ministry will look very different from one context to another.

At the same time, lists can be helpful for organizing strategies and expectations. When you provide people with a list, they are far more likely to move in the desired direction. Plus, if they don't move toward those expectations, it's easier to identify the specific points where they are falling short. God himself uses lists. He expressed his holiness through a list of 613 statutes in the books of Moses which were signified in Ten Commandments, summarized in two commandments, and fulfilled in the flesh of the one mediator, Jesus Christ (Matt. 22:34–40; John 1:1, 14; Rom. 7:12; 10:4; James 2:10).

And so, despite my queasiness about lists, I am about to provide a list of three practices that your ministry can help parents implement in their homes, as well as one practice that you'll pursue alongside families in your church. Here's my list of family practices that mark family-equipping ministries. The ministry equips parents to engage in (1) faith talks, (2) faith walks, (3) faith processes in their homes, and (4) to become families in faith for spiritual orphans.

But I warn you: Don't call me to tell me what wasn't on the list. If you do, I'm likely to say to you what I said to my first-grader several years ago: "Life isn't about lists; it's about doing what's right wherever you are. You didn't—and there will be consequences." You are responsible to look for the unique ways that the gospel applies in the lives of families wherever God has placed you.

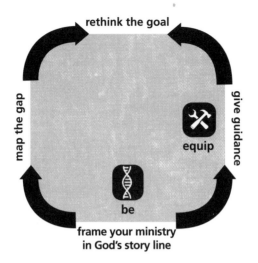

PREPARING PARENTS TO LEAD FAITH TALKS

Parents are the primary teachers in their children's lives, even if they don't know it. Some parents are better teachers than others, but every parent is a teacher when it comes to the children with whom he or she shares a home. Even after decades of family fragmentation, the most significant influence on children's spiritual formation remains "the religious life modeled and taught to them by their parents."[1] The problem is, many churches have provided parents with the impression that when it comes to shaping their children's souls, the primary teachers ought to be paid professionals at church.

That's not the story that the Scriptures tell us, though. In his letter to the Ephesians, Paul specifically commanded fathers not simply to be good examples for their children but to provide their children with training (*paideia*) "of the Lord" (Eph. 6:4). The meaning of the term that Paul connected here to the training of children includes planned and intentional teaching of particular content. Paul later used the same word to describe the function of Scripture in a pastor's leadership of a local church (2 Tim. 3:16–17).

Early Christians clearly understood the practical implications of Paul's words. A sermon from the late first century A.D. admonishes parents to make certain their children "receive the instruction that is in Christ." A letter written to the church in the ancient city of Philadelphia specifically calls fathers to teach their children "the Holy Scriptures as well as trades." In a second-century trial that resulted in the martyrdom of several Christians, the Roman governor asked a Christian named Paeon who had taught him about Jesus. Paeon responded, "I received from my parents this good confession." Another Christian immediately chimed in, "I did indeed listen gladly to the words of Justin [a famous Christian philosopher], but I too received the Christian faith through my parents."[2]

Consider for a moment the words of these early Christians. When asked who had taught the Christian faith to them, their first and immediate response was "my parents." They had learned theology from Justin, the premier Christian philosopher of his generation. Yet they identified their parents as the people who had taught them God's truth.

If youth or children in your church were asked the same sort of question, how would they respond? To be sure, they would recognize their parents as significant influences in their lives. But would they identify their parents as the primary people who are teaching them the truths of God?

Faith Talk: Designated time, at least once per week, for the household to gather for prayer and to study a biblical truth together. This household gathering may include not only parents and children but also other individuals who have been invited to share this time with the family.

In my research, only one-third of churched parents read or discussed Scripture with their children at least once a week. If that's the predominant pattern, it seems unlikely that the typical teenager in an evangelical church would identify his or her parents first as teachers of God's Word. The more likely response to the question, "Who taught you?" might be the youth minister, a group of Christian friends, perhaps even a Christian author or musician. When it comes to teaching God's Word and ways, parents have slipped into a supporting role. Earlier generations of Christians understood what contemporary Christians seem to have missed: Families are the first and most effective small group of all, and every parent is a teacher.

WHY FAITH TALKS?

The purpose of faith talks is to restore Christian parents to their God-ordained role as teachers of God's Word in their children's lives. Your ministry may choose some term other than *faith talks*, of course. *Family devotions* might communicate the point more clearly in your context; somewhere else, you could go with *family faith training* or even *family time* or *family night* as the best description for a faith talk. *Family worship* is a time-tested phrase from the Puritans. I used that term for several years until I found out that, in the minds of a few parents, *family worship* implied leading a miniature church service in their house, complete with hymnals and liturgy! Since then, I've steered away from calling congregants to engage in family worship. In a few congregations, the venerable title *family altar* still makes sense. And yet, confronted with the idea of an altar for their family, contemporary families are less likely to think about teaching Scripture and more likely to wonder whether their neighborhoods are zoned for animal sacrifices.

The name that you assign to faith talks is negotiable; the practice behind the name is not. For parents to become primary disciple-makers in their children's lives, they must become Bible teachers in their homes. This is not to suggest that Christian parents should become their children's sole instructors in Scripture. After all, the Great Commission to make disciples was given to the whole church as a calling to reach the whole world, including children (Matt. 28:19). Every Christian parent should, however, become a significant and consistent conveyor of God's Word in his or her children's lives.

Unfortunately, when it comes to coaching their children in the truths of God, many parents have no idea where to begin—perhaps, in part, because their churches have provided little training and no accountability for such a task. That's why family-equipping ministry is so crucial. Church leaders who effectively equip families understand that one essential component in preparing God's people for works of ministry (Eph. 4:12) is training parents to teach their children.

Real-Life Ideas for Moving from Expecting to Equipping

Faith Talk Idea: Develop a weekly, family faith talk guide for parents and provide it in such a way that any parent who regularly attends worship or Bible study for a few weeks will repeatedly see and hear about it.

WHY WEEKLY?

Here's a simple expectation that I have seen effectively implemented in a significant number of churches: Parents choose a time once each week to lead a family faith talk. The church encourages the parents, holds them accountable, and provides them with resources for this weekly faith talk.

Why only once a week? I claim no infallible rationale for leading a family faith talk once a week. If you or your ministry leaders want to encourage family devotions more often than weekly, that's something to discuss with God and to adapt to your particular context.

Still, I like the idea of a once-per-week pattern. I like this because it's rooted in the rhythms of creation itself (Ex. 20:11; 31:17), because it can reflect at home the celebration of Christ's resurrection that happens every week at church (Luke 24:1; Acts 20:7), and because weeks mark times of worship and ritual throughout the Scriptures (Ex. 34:22; Lev. 23:15; Deut. 16:9–10). I also find once a week to be sufficiently frequent to make faith talks a habit but not so frequent that parents become burdened with unrealistic expectations if they have never engaged in faith talks before. In many households, weekly faith talks eventually develop into daily family devotions.

PROVIDING THE TOOLS THAT PARENTS NEED

So where do you begin when it comes to equipping parents for weekly faith talks? First off, don't schedule any new programs or events to equip parents to lead faith talks. The parents that show up at such events are typically those who are already doing what you want to equip them to do. The ones who actually need the equipping will find somewhere else to be.

What's far more important than creating a program is providing a tool. Develop a weekly family faith talk guide for parents and make certain that they cannot regularly attend church without seeing and hearing about this tool. The family faith talk guide must be clear, brief, and adaptable to a variety of circumstances. The outline could be as simple as a fun activity for the whole family, followed by a Scripture, a few discussion questions, and a closing prayer.

In some congregations, this tool may be provided in the form of a faith talk outline on the slideshow screen at the end of each week's worship celebration. The outline can be reinforced by providing the same outline on an index card in the bulletin. In another context, such as a youth or children's ministry, it may be more effective to include faith talk guides in a weekly or monthly e-mail blast to the parents. Some churches use their monthly church newsletter to provide these tools. Others distribute and discuss the family faith talk guides through their weekly small groups.

Regardless of how you provide faith talk guides to families in your church, connect the church and the home by coordinating the faith talk guides with other teachings that are happening in the church. Many ministries develop their weekly guides from the same theme or Scripture text as the pastor's message. Others base their faith talk tools on Sunday school lessons.

Once the family faith talk guide becomes a natural part of your ministry, use these guides to begin intentional training for parents. Again, don't launch any new programs! Use current practices in your congregation as catalysts for equipping parents to lead faith talks. Do you have a monthly parents' meeting for your youth or children's ministry? Maybe you have a men's Bible study or a women's prayer group? What about adult Sunday school? Do you have small groups that meet in homes during the week? Look for opportunities for you or another ministry leader to train participants in these activities on how to lead a family faith talk.

Don't assume too much, though. For many parents, the idea of family faith talk is so foreign that you will need to engage in very basic dialogue for them even to understand what this might look like. You may have to start simpler than you ever imagined. What I am proposing here is radically countercultural—not only counter to the world's culture but also to the culture of many churches.

In one church, the pastor was struggling to implement family faith talks at mealtimes. When he spoke with parents, it became clear that most of the congregants had never even eaten a family meal together with all media turned off. Sometimes for a generation or more, family members had eaten separately, or they took their meals in front of the television. As a result, they could not even grasp what it might look like to gather for a family Bible study. And so, the church decided to take some radical steps to reverse this trend: Once a month, the congregation replaced their evening worship service with a family dinner time. (Notice that they didn't launch a new program; they shifted the function of an existing time slot.) During these times, the church filled the fellowship hall with family-sized tables and placed families together. Children whose parents were not present were placed with families whose parents were there. No video clips or worship songs were presented during the meal—the point was to practice something at church that could be replicated at home. The pastor simply provided a family devotional guide and stood up from time to time to make a suggestion about what to discuss next. In this way, the church developed disciple-making habits in Christian households, showed families a new way to do life, and (when some unbelieving families began to attend) presented a clear witness to the power of the gospel to transform homes.

It may take your congregation a year or more before family faith talks become a normal part of people's lives. Even then, many families will still struggle. Respond to these families in light of the gospel that brings us together as brothers and sisters—a gospel wherein all is done as a free and joyous response to God's finished work in Jesus Christ.

IT IS HARD, AND YOU ARE INADEQUATE

After I presented some of these strategies in one congregation, one very kind and sincere lady responded, "I want to see this happen in our church; I want to see it happen in my home. But our church has never even suggested anything like this to anyone before. The transition looks so hard. And I don't know about anyone else, but I feel so inadequate."

"I want to provide you with a word of encouragement," I said. "It is hard; you are inadequate; and so am I."

Responses like that probably explain why encouragement never shows up on my spiritual gift inventory. But I stand by my statement, though perhaps

I should have said it a bit more gently. And I did go on to explain more about what I meant: Transformations of this sort are hard, and we are inadequate. That's why God sent his Son to redeem us and his Spirit to reside within us. If you want to move your ministry toward family-equipping, remember that the same Spirit who is transforming you is also present in the life of every other believer. Trust the power of God's Spirit and the proclamation of God's Word to bring transformation in the lives of God's people. Don't focus on family-equipping, center your life and ministry on the Equipper. That's the key to a family-equipping ministry that lasts.

REAL-LIFE IDEAS FOR MOVING FROM EXPECTING TO EQUIPPING

Sample Family Faith Talk Guide

This is a sample from a series of family faith talk guides I developed for ministries that are moving toward family-equipping.

"Be Together" asks each family member to bring a specific object to talk about and provides a beginning point for discussion.

"Think Together" provides one paragraph that connects with the message from the previous Sunday, as well as a specific thought for each age-group.

"Listen Together" is a brief Scripture reading with three discussion questions.

"Go Together" provides a faith walk idea to reinforce the central truth throughout the week, "when you sit in your house, and when you walk by the way, and when you lie down, and when you rise" (Deut. 6:7 ESV).

Many congregations are now using this same outline to develop their own faith talk guides.

WORKING TOGETHER AS GOD'S PEOPLE: A FAITH TALK ABOUT THE CHURCH

Be Together

Ask each person to bring to family faith talk an item that represents his or her favorite sports team or something that reminds him or her of a favorite team activity. Allow each person to share what he or she likes best about that team or activity. Talk specifically about how people work together in this sport or activity.

Think Together

If someone is a Christian, God has given that person the gift of Jesus himself; God has made that person right with himself through the perfect goodness of Jesus. All by itself, that would be unspeakably wonderful! But the gift of Jesus also results in the gift of God's Holy Spirit in us. The Holy Spirit joins us with other believers and works in us to make us more like Jesus. In response to this gift of God, believers practice fellowship with other believers, join with other believers

continued

REAL-LIFE IDEAS FOR MOVING FROM EXPECTING TO EQUIPPING *continued*

to proclaim the gospel to all people, and seek peace in their communities and in every part of God's creation. The people who join together in God's work in a particular place are known as the church. The church is a team that works together, but it is a team with a task that is far more important than any sports team. What joins the church together is not a certain uniform or hope for victory. The Spirit of God himself is what ties the church together.

With younger children, make certain they understand that the church is not the building where you meet to worship. The church is the people of God.

With older children, use this catechism question and answer: What is the visible church? The visible church is the organized society of professing believers in all ages and places wherein the gospel is truly preached and the ordinances of baptism and the Lord's Supper are administered in true faith. Have fun with catechism. For example, let the children quiz mom or dad on the answer this week.

With teenagers, talk about how God can work through the church even though the church is filled with imperfect people.

Listen Together

Read Ephesians 4:11–16. Paul did not originally write this letter to one individual Christian or even to all Christians everywhere. This letter was sent to a particular group of believers or a group of churches in one place. It was important to Paul not only that individual Christians believed the truth about God but also that believers responded rightly to God's grace by working together with other believers around them.

Who are the pastors in our church (4:11)?

Why have these pastors been appointed (4:12)? Sometimes, people think that the pastors are supposed to do all the work of the church. That is not true. The pastors equip one another and the rest of the church to do what needs to be done, to build up the whole church. That's teamwork!

In this "teamwork," what should be our family's goal (4:12–13)? What does our family do to join in God's work of guiding the church toward unity and maturity? Is there anything we should be doing that we are not doing right now?

Go Together: Faith Walk

After this week's family faith talk, locate a list of your church's pastors or other leaders. Print the list and post it on the refrigerator. Bake some cookies with your children this week. As you work together, talk about how everyone in your family is working together as a team to make the cookies. Talk about how our pastors help all of us in the church to work together as a team. After you slide the cookies in the oven, spend a few moments praying for the pastors of your church. Chances are, your family doesn't really need all the cookies. So wrap up a few for a neighbor and include an invitation to come to church. Or, take some to one of the pastors for whom you prayed this week. Take the cookies as a family and talk more about how God's Spirit works in us so that we can work together.

FAMILY-EQUIPPING TRANSITION 2B: EQUIP FAMILIES FOR FAITH WALKS AND FAITH PROCESSES

The next two practices—faith walks and faith processes—build on the foundation of family faith talks. Faith talks focus on teaching God's Word "diligently to your children" (Deut. 6:7 ESV). Faith walks and faith processes fulfill the next portion of God's Word spoken through Moses. The law giver of Israel commanded God's people to converse about God's truth "when you sit in your house, and when you walk by the way, and when you lie down, and when you rise" (Deut. 6:7 ESV).

PREPARING FAMILIES FOR FAITH WALKS

Faith walks don't require a separate program or even a slot on the church calendar. Faith walks are simply a category to describe conversations about God that unfold in the context of your day-by-day life. It's the discussion about different views of creation as you stroll through the zoo. It's the conversation about how God can allow evil in the world that comes as the strobing ambulance lights around a roadside wreck fade in the rearview mirror. It's the question about whether Jesus is the only way to heaven that pops up at the dinner table after your child befriends a Hindu classmate. Every question that arises in the daily walk of life is an opportunity for parents to form their child's faith.

Faith Walk: A discussion in the course of daily life that turns a child's attention toward the presence of the gospel and the providence of God in every part of life.

Brian Haynes, a family-equipping pastor in Texas, has dubbed faith walks "God moments" and "God sightings." In another context, I have described faith walks as part of the ongoing process of sensing God's presence "in the hullabaloo"—in the hustle and bustle of daily life.[1]

Whatever you call faith walks in your particular context, the aim remains the same: Faith walk moments remind us that because God is working all things together for the good of those who love him, even the most mundane events of life can call attention to God's glory and his story.

You can't plan or program faith walks; they are spontaneous by their very nature. What you can do is prepare parents to take advantage of these opportunities when they do happen.

REAL-LIFE IDEAS FOR MOVING FROM EXPECTING TO EQUIPPING

The point of these ideas is not to provide a step-by-step guide to making the shift from expecting to equipping. The point is to spark your thinking by providing you with examples of real-life practices that other ministries have used effectively.

IDEAS FOR DEVELOPING FAITH WALK HABITS IN THE FAMILIES OF YOUR CHURCH

Include Faith Walk Ideas in Your Faith Talk Guide

In each weekly faith talk guide, suggest a faith walk activity—something in ordinary daily life that parents can easily turn toward a discussion of God's truth. Parents may not use every particular activity that you provide, but these suggestions will remind parents to look for faith walk opportunities in every area of life.

Include Faith Walk Testimonies in Church Newsletters and Blogs

When a parent shares a faith walk testimony with you—not simply a cute anecdote, but an authentic discussion with a child that turned toward God's story—ask the parent if you may share the testimony in the church newsletter or on the website.

Equip Parents for Daily Prayers with Their Children

Help parents to see the significance of praying with each child each morning and night. For many children and parents, evening prayer time in particular provides an opportunity to discuss God's truth by reflecting on the day together. Provide parents with written prayers and blessings for their children, if this would be helpful in your context.

continued

REAL-LIFE IDEAS FOR MOVING FROM EXPECTING TO EQUIPPING continued

Equip Parents with Discussion Questions about Their Family's Entertainment
Provide parents with lists of specific questions to discuss with their children after listening to music together or watching a movie or television program. For example, here are five questions that might be asked after every movie and provided to parents as a handout: Where did this movie tell the truth about what is right and good? Where did this movie tell lies about what is right and good? What actions in this story should we try to copy? Which ones should we avoid? In what ways did the person who made this movie, perhaps without even knowing it, include reflections of God's story line?

Train Parents to See Their Children's Questions as God-Given Opportunities
Train parents to think in terms of this axiom: Every question that my child asks is an opportunity for me to help my child see all of life in light of God's story line. In the Old Testament, Moses and Joshua prepared parents to recount the story of God's work with Israel in response to their children's questions (Ex. 13:14–16; Deut. 6:20–25; Josh. 4:6–8, 21–24). Before they answer any question from their child, encourage parents to ask themselves, "How can I answer this question in a way that calls attention to the story of creation and fall, redemption and consummation?"

Train Teachers and Ministry Leaders to Share Faith Walk Testimonies
Work with teachers and ministry leaders, whenever a child asks an important spiritual question at church, to share the discussion with parents and to speak in terms of having a "God sighting" or faith walk with their child. Encourage parents to look for opportunities to continue the faith walk discussion at home.

PREPARING FAMILIES FOR FAITH PROCESSES

Faith grows. Or at least, it should.

The apostles once implored their Lord, "Increase our faith!" (Luke 17:5). And no wonder. According to the teachings that the apostles had heard from the lips of Jesus, it was possible for faith to blossom from an almost imperceptible speck—"as small as a mustard seed"—into an earthshaking force (Matt. 17:20; Luke 17:6). The apostles had listened as Jesus praised "great faith" (Matt. 8:10; 15:28; Luke 7:9) and then as he rebuked his followers for their "little faith" (Matt. 6:30; 8:26; 14:31; 16:8; Luke 12:28). From the perspective of the inspired authors who proclaimed the gospel in the decades after the resurrection of Jesus, growth in faith was both desired (2 Cor. 10:15; Eph. 4:13–14; 2 Thess. 1:3) and expected (Heb. 5:11—6:2).

There's a particular challenge when guiding children to grow in their faith, though: The precise processes of growth in faith can be very different from one child to another. This has as much to do with children's differing patterns of social and intellectual development as with their spiritual formation. Even for the best parents, it is difficult to address each child's individual spiritual challenges in a weekly faith talk. That's why family-equipping ministries partner with parents to develop specific faith processes for each child. The central aim of a faith process is for parents to be able to answer one simple question regarding each of their children: What needs to happen next in this child's spiritual growth?

In some churches, the faith process for children might look like a series of passages from one stage of life to the next. Brian Haynes has pioneered this approach in what he calls "legacy milestones," a comprehensive partnership with parents to aim their child stage-by-stage toward Christian maturity.[2]

The ordinances of the church—baptism and the Lord's Supper—are typically preceded by personal preparation and marked by a celebration that draws the faith community together (Acts 2:38–47; 1 Cor. 11:17–34). While recognizing that rites of passage are not equivalent to the sacraments or ordinances of the church, legacy milestones follow a similar pattern of preparation and celebration. Prior to each passage, the church provides parents with materials and training to guide their child toward a specific set of Christ-centered perspectives and practices for that stage of life. The child's movement toward deeper faith is then celebrated with the entire community of faith.

Particularly in the Old Testament, memorable moments with God might be marked by the building of a altar or the stacking of stones; in many cases, the family or faith community rallied around this monument to celebrate God's work among them (Gen. 12:8; 26:25; 35:7; Ex. 17:15; Josh. 4:1–7; 22:34). In a similar way, each passage in a child's life is marked by a specific, memorable milestone celebration that brings the family and faith community together. For some rites of passage, this might look like a road trip with mom and dad to a designated destination, preceded by specific instruction and aimed toward a threshold moment in the child's life. Baptism may mark the milestone of baby dedication in some congregations and of the child's profession of faith in others. In some cases, a particular token (an engraved sword, for example, to mark a boy's transition to manhood, or a special Bible to remember the date of one's baptism, or a framed letter from parents or a significant mentor at another milestone) may be provided to remind children of these celebrations. The giving of a purity ring might mark the child's commitment to remain a virgin until marriage.

REAL-LIFE IDEAS FOR MOVING FROM EXPECTING TO EQUIPPING

Legacy Milestones Faith Process

Milestone 1—Parent and Child Dedication: Prior to dedicating newly born or newly adopted children, train parents to begin family faith talks even if their children are infants. Celebrate the parents' commitment in a public worship celebration.

Milestone 2—Profession of Faith: Prepare parents to be the persons who guide their children to faith in Jesus Christ. Celebrate the child's personal profession of faith through baptism (if your congregation practices believers' baptism), first Communion, or some other celebration that the entire faith community shares.

Milestone 3—Preparing for Adolescence: Prepare parents to talk openly about adolescence and God's design for human sexuality with their children. Help parents to plan a road trip or some other outing with their child—fathers with sons, mothers with daughters—that celebrates God's work in the growing child.

Milestone 4—Purity for Life: Offer a seminar that prepares parents to guide their teenager toward a gospel-centered perspective on relating to the opposite sex. Celebrate the teenager's commitment to remain a virgin until marriage with the gift of a purity ring.

Milestone 5—Passage to Adulthood: Equip parents to train their children extensively in the basic truths of the Christian faith and in what it means to be an adult. When the adolescent has achieved certain core competencies, parents celebrate a passage to adulthood, with new roles and expectations for their son or daughter.

Milestone 6—High School Graduation: Equip parents to train their children in Christian apologetics. The celebration of this milestone is linked to high school graduation and includes a parental blessing of the son or daughter.

Milestone 7—Lifetime in Christ: The son or daughter takes on a responsibility to live as a disciple maker, developing habits of prayer, Scripture study, deeper faith, obedience to God's calling, generosity, and continuing in Christian community.

For more information, see http://www.legacymilestones.com.

Adapted from materials developed by Brian Haynes

Another way of helping parents develop a faith process with their children is simply to equip them to invest individual discipleship time with each of their children on a consistent basis. During these times, parents might spend a few moments in the Scriptures with the child and then consider questions such as, "What has God been doing in your life this week? What needs to happen next in your life as a follower of Jesus? What struggles are you facing right now?" For children who have not yet become believers, a weekly meeting of this sort will most likely be when and where the child first professes faith in Jesus Christ. Prepare parents to be the people who lead their children to trust Jesus in the context of these faith processes.

Faith Process: A plan that involves parents in a child's spiritual growth by partnering with parents to address the child's particular needs at each stage of life.

One day a week, I take each of my daughters to a local café for a snack, a brief Bible study, and lots of talking about life—Hannah in the morning and Skylar in the afternoon. Each of them has a faith process journal where they record a few sentences each week to remember our discussion as well as a Bible verse and a prayer. These times together are very different because my daughters are at different places in their spiritual development. I am not yet certain that Skylar has professed authentic faith in Jesus, while Hannah is deeply wrestling with issues like the eternal status of Native Americans who died before the gospel reached North America. Skylar is learning the first lines of the Apostles' Creed and looking at the life of Jesus; Hannah and I are working verse by verse through the book of Acts.

What I do with Hannah and Skylar is not complicated, and it only takes three hours or so each week, but every week each girl eagerly anticipates her time of focused discussion and discipleship. Admittedly, the child's anticipation could have something to do with the privilege of selecting the bagel and caffeinated beverage of her choice—but as I watch them grow, I can't help but think that faith is somehow at work in all of this too.

While the particular locations and terminology may differ from generation to generation, developing a personal faith process with each of your children is not a new concept. In fact, I developed the idea for what I do with my girls from the practices of a devout eighteenth-century mother who raised ten children. Susanna Wesley, the mother of John and Charles Wesley, set aside a specific time each week to disciple each of her children. John's designated time was Thursday evening, and the long-term effect on his life was momentous.[3]

Once again, churches do not need to start any new programs to equip parents for faith processes. Instead, use Bible study times, Sunday school classes, and small groups that are already in place. Include preparation for faith processes in weekly faith talk outlines. Work faith process suggestions into men's breakfasts, parent's day out orientations, and preparations for child dedications. If you want to assess whether what you're doing is working, randomly ask a few faithful parents, "What specifically needs to happen next in your child's spiritual development?" If their response is vague or focused on external behaviors, it may be a signal that the practice of a faith process isn't quite clear to them yet.

REAL-LIFE IDEAS FOR MOVING FROM EXPECTING TO EQUIPPING

Ideas for a Weekly Faith Process

1. Choose an enjoyable place to be together; if possible, make it a weekly tradition where your child goes somewhere or orders some menu item that he or she can't at any other time. Consider having a special journal that is used only for your weekly faith process.
2. Choose a book of the Bible, a particular biblical text, or a creed that you will work on little by little over many weeks; the time spent together is more important than how many words or verses you cover each week. By choosing a book of the Bible or a creed, you do not have to figure out what to do each week; simply pick up where you left off the week before.
3. Read the Scripture or creed together.
4. Discuss: "What did this mean to people back then? What should this mean for us today?"
5. Ask: "What has God been doing in your life this week? What struggles are you facing right now? How does the gospel apply to these struggles? What needs to happen next in your life to follow Jesus more closely?" Be willing to share your own answers to these questions too, confessing your sins to one another (James 5:16–18).
6. Together, write in the journal a one-sentence thought, a Scripture verse from today's discussion, and a brief prayer.

DEVELOPING FAMILIES IN FAITH FOR THOSE WHO ARE FAR

Care for orphans is essential to our identity in Jesus Christ. Believers in Jesus Christ are all, after all, ex-orphans adopted by God's grace. That's why James, the son of Joseph and Mary, whose half brother Jesus had been adopted by Joseph, declared that "undefiled religion" requires God's children to act decisively on behalf of "orphans and widows in their distress" (James 1:27 NASB). God's concern for orphans didn't begin with these words from James, though. God's plan to rescue the fatherless through his people began long before Jesus set foot on Earth.

Seven times in the law that God gave to the Israelite people, Moses reiterated Israel's responsibility to care for the fatherless (Ex. 22:22–24; Deut. 10:18; 14:29; 16:11–14; 24:17–21; 26:12–13; 27:19). "Have I been stingy with my food and refused to share it with orphans?" righteous Job asked, "No, from childhood I have cared for orphans like a father. . . . If I raised my hand against an orphan . . . then let my shoulder be wrenched out of place!" (Job 31:17–18, 21–22 NLT). When the nation of Israel failed to care for orphans in the Old Testament (Isa. 1:17), the Lord declared through Isaiah, "Your new moons and your appointed feasts my soul hates . . . When you spread out your hands, I will hide my eyes from you; even though you make many prayers, I will not listen" (Isa. 1:14–15 ESV).

With this in mind, suppose that your ministry developed the finest church-based training for faith talks and faith walks—so thorough and comprehensive that every member of your church began to participate. And suppose that milestone celebrations clearly marked every child's faith process.

But what if you did all of this in such a way that children from fractured families and abusive homes were not part of your church's vision? You aren't telling these families that they can't be involved, of course. Your church has simply decided to focus on a different demographic, one with a believing mom and dad in every household and no recent visits from the Department of Human Services. After all, wouldn't people from families like *that* be more comfortable with people like *them*?

What would be God's perspective on such a family ministry?

I think his response might run something like this: "Your faith talks and faith walks, my soul hates. When you celebrate your milestones, I hide my eyes from you. Though you speak much about families, I will not listen." If our religious rituals do not drive us to care for those that don't fit easily into our faith communities, God despises our rituals and turns his face from our prayers.

Seen in relation to Jesus, not only the children of believers but also the children of unbelievers—anyone, in fact, who "does the will" of our Father in heaven—may become our sisters, brothers, fathers, and mothers in Christ (Matt. 12:48–50; 1 Tim. 5:1–2). That's because faith in Jesus flows through divine adoption, not through anyone's earthly heritage. The gospel of Jesus Christ cuts through any privilege that we may perceive we have because of pedigrees or family trees and hurls these prideful pretensions into the fires of divine judgment (Matt. 3:7–10; Luke 3:7–9).

And so, in light of this calling to care for orphans, what about spiritual orphans—the children whose parents aren't yet believers in Jesus Christ? Where do these children fit in a family-equipping ministry? The answer is simple: The gospel compels Christians around them to become their families. That's why family-equipping must include the equipping of families in faith—mature believers who mentor spiritual orphans, who celebrate milestones with the children whose parents are not yet believers, and who seek opportunities to share the gospel with unbelieving parents.

Families in faith are not an afterthought in a family-equipping ministry. Because family-equipping is rooted in the story line of God and centered in the gospel of Jesus Christ, functioning as a family in faith is one of the most crucial roles in this ministry. This is one of many key areas where singles and senior adults make vital contributions to family-equipping ministry.

If any family ministry fails to reach the spiritual orphans all around us, such ministry is not family ministry at all; it is family idolatry. And the idolization of family is no less despicable in God's sight than the Asherah poles of Iron Age Israel or the pantheon of ancient Rome. Families in faith are your defense against family idolatry.

As a family-equipping minister, select families in faith carefully, train them well, and provide clear expectations for their role in children's lives. Match particular children with members of these families in faith. Celebrate volunteers' contributions as frequently as possible. Without the contributions of families in faith, family-equipping can quickly become so focused on "you and your children" that it fails to touch the lives of those "who are far off" (Acts 2:39).

FAMILY-EQUIPPING TRANSITION 3: ACKNOWLEDGE

Moses knew he was about to die when he spoke the words that have been preserved for us in the book of Deuteronomy. Soon, he would pass from this life, and a new leader would take the tribes of Israel into the land of promise. Moses did not speak these last words frivolously or lightly. And yet, as he spoke, Moses reiterated seven different variations of a single clause: "Take care . . . lest you forget the things that your eyes have seen" (Deut. 4:9, 23; 6:12; 8:11, 14, 19; 9:7 ESV).

Moses was not simply telling the Israelites to tuck a recollection of God's works somewhere in the back of their minds. Moses was reminding his people to live constantly in light of what God had accomplished to redeem them. And what was the means for maintaining these memories in the lives of God's people? "Teach them," Moses declared, "to your children and to their children after them" (Deut. 4:9).

Yet why did Moses repeat this clause "lest you forget" so many times? His mind was far from senile! Even at 120 years old, "his eye was undimmed, and his vigor unabated" (Deut. 34:7 ESV).

Moses repeated these Spirit-inspired words seven times for a reason.

The primary reason for these words from Moses was to point the people toward their need for a word from God more memorable than any law that Moses had spoken. This consummate Word would be a person, not a principle, and his work would be unforgettably engraved in his people's

"Over-communicate your family-equipping approach at every level of church life! From the pulpit all the way down to the pre-camp parent meeting, use every opportunity and venue you have available to you to promote the coordination of church and family. Develop statements that clarify your goal. Many churches even weave the message into their mission statements: 'Changing our world for Christ, one home at a time' or 'Where faith meets home,' for example. Be creative with your approaches, remembering that people need to hear or see something several times before it sinks in."
—Jay Strother

very hearts (Jer. 31:31–34; Ezek. 36:24–27). All of Scripture is about Jesus—even these commands from Moses to the Israelites to remember God's works (John 5:46; Luke 24:27).

But there is a secondary principle at work in this text too: Every one of us is prone to forget the implications of what God has done for us and in us. Simply put, we need constant reminders so that we will remember what God desires to do among us—and one habit of life that grows out of remembering what God has done among us is the training of children in his ways. Without constant reminders, we are prone to forget this implication of God's work among us.

That's why family-equipping ministries must mention God's expectations for families far more often than the yearly couples' retreat, Mother's Day, Father's Day, and baby dedication Sunday. Ministries that have effectively transitioned to family-equipping ministry constantly acknowledge the role of parents as disciple-making partners in their children's lives. Without constant reminders, we are prone to forget what it means to live as sons and daughters of God, as brothers and sisters of Jesus himself, and as potential brothers and sisters of our children (Heb. 12:5).

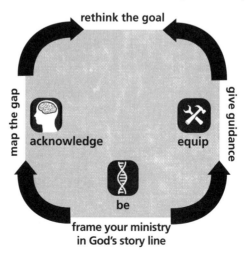

HOW LONG DOES IT TAKE TO SEE THE CONNECTION?

For family-equipping practices to work their way into the daily lives of families, it isn't enough to acknowledge parents as primary disciple-makers only at occasional family events. Hints of this role must make appearances in the everyday life, work, and literature of the church, in such places as the weekly worship folder, illustrations in the pastor's message, the announcement slides before the worship service, the times of prayer that precede the Sunday school lesson, and small group discussion guides. This does not mean that family-equipping should become the controlling theme in these resources, but it must be consistently acknowledged as one aspect of how your community of faith responds to the gospel together.

Do you want to know how effectively your church is acknowledging the role of parents? Here's a question that is worth asking: "How long could someone be involved in this congregation before realizing that one implication of God's work among us is that parents should become disciple-making brothers and sisters in their children's lives?"

To find an answer to this question, imagine that you have never heard about parents' primary responsibility for the spiritual formation of their children. Now, imagine that you begin to attend your congregation. Look at your ministry website. Think through the materials that people receive through your ministry each week. Listen carefully during Sunday worship celebrations, and flip through the church newsletter. If it's possible to attend your congregation for more than a week or two without clearly recognizing the responsibility of parents to disciple their children, consider how you might communicate this vision more clearly and frequently. Never assume that parents will know or remember their divinely designated roles; constantly acknowledge parents in a variety of venues as primary disciple-makers in their children's lives.

This pattern of constant acknowledgment occurs at the same time as the equipping that I described in the previous couple of chapters. Without equipping, constant acknowledgment of parents' responsibilities will result only in feelings of guilt. But, without acknowledgment at every level of the church's life and work, equipping is likely to reach only the families that are already engaged in discipleship practices with their children. For habits of family discipleship to reach beyond a small handful of particularly faithful families, everyone must hear the message over and over.

REAL-LIFE IDEAS FOR MOVING FROM ASSUMING TO ACKNOWLEDGING

The point of these ideas is not to provide a step-by-step guide to making the shift from assuming to acknowledging. The point is to spark your thinking by providing you with examples of real-life practices that other ministries have used effectively. No new programs were put into place in any of these examples; existing ministries were reoriented and coordinated to acknowledge the primary role of parents in discipleship.

Acknowledge Family-Equipping with the "Newlies"

Include faith talk training and teaching about the role of parents in three key life transitions: (1) Newlyweds—Your church probably already requires premarital counseling before weddings that your pastors conduct. Include a session in premarital counseling that acknowledges parents as primary disciple-makers and equips newly married couples to begin faith talks together. (2) Newborns and newly adopted—Your church probably already dedicates or baptizes newborns and newly adopted children. Require a series of classes before the dedication or baptism. Include childcare tips and training in these classes, but focus on acknowledgment of parents as primary disciple-makers and on training families for faith talks, faith walks, and faith processes. (3) New members—Your church probably already requires new members to attend a series of classes. Dedicate one of these sessions to acknowledging God's design for families, with an emphasis on the role of parents as primary disciple-makers.

Acknowledge Expectations for Parents at Orientations

Before camps or mission trips, you probably already schedule orientations for parents. During these orientations, mention the expectation for parents to serve as primary disciple-makers and to lead faith talks, faith walks, and faith processes.

Acknowledge the Role of Parents in Weekly Worship Folders and Small Group Discussion Guides

Include a brief paragraph in these materials that explains why, from a biblical perspective, parents are primary disciple-makers. Include specific statements about the church's expectations for practices and processes of family discipleship.

Acknowledge the Possibilities for Family Discipleship Through Testimonies

If you know parents who have recently started family faith talks, provide opportunities for them to give a brief testimony in Sunday morning worship about their movement toward becoming disciple-makers in their children's lives.

continued

REAL-LIFE IDEAS FOR MOVING FROM ASSUMING TO ACKNOWLEDGING *continued*

Acknowledge Parents' Needs and Responsibilities through Deacon Ministry
Work with your deacons so that they develop habits of faith talks and faith walks in their households. Assign a dozen church families to each deacon in your church. Work with the deacons so that each deacon schedules a time with one of these families every month. The result will be that every family in your church receives at least one deacon visit in their home each year. A key part of each visit should be to ask how the family is doing when it comes to family faith talks. Equip deacons to offer assistance and resources if families are struggling in this area.

Acknowledge the Need of Generations for One Another
Scripture repeatedly emphasizes the need for younger generations to respect and learn from older ones (Lev. 19:32; 1 Kings 12:6–15; 1 Tim. 5:1–16). Yet, in many contemporary churches, the generations never interact with one another. In some cases, generations are even segregated in different worship celebrations. In the ways that you speak and in your emphases in printed materials, repeatedly mention the need for intergenerational integration and appreciation. If possible, eliminate generationally segregated worship services.

SAY IT, THEN SAY IT AGAIN— AND AGAIN AND AGAIN

Churches in the segmented-programmatic model have typically attempted to acknowledge the role of parents through occasional events and activities like a half-hour breakout session at the marriage retreat, an emotional plea during a special sermon series, a stadium event to challenge men, or a mother-daughter conference for women.

So what's the problem with promoting family ministry through events?

There's not one. But acknowledging parents through such occasional promotions will never be enough.

Think of it this way: Do you recall your toughest subject in middle school or high school? Let's suppose that instead of spending time week by

"Why aren't churches acknowledging parents as disciple-makers in their children's lives? I think it's because we have retreated from holding anyone in our churches accountable—including parents—and because it's not in our job descriptions. But I think there's another reason too: We as ministers like to be needed for our programming for children and youth; we fear that, if we acknowledge parents as disciple-makers in their children's lives, our activities and programs might not be necessary anymore. Our identities have become too bound up in the programming that we produce."

—Tim Brown

> "If parents are the primary disciple-makers, every ministry and leader exists to support but never to replace the parents' role. A key objective for the entire church must be to equip and support parents in making their homes ministry centers for the spiritual growth of their children. In our church, we communicate this message church-wide through every venue, all the way from Sunday sermons to the monthly coffee that's hosted for expectant mothers—we want them to get the message even before their baby is born!"
>
> —Jay Strother

week in that course, everything was crammed into a couple of high-energy weekend events each year. Even if you had the maturity of an adult, how well would you have learned the material?

No matter how well-produced these learning events might have been and no matter how deeply the events may have moved you, you would not have adequately mastered the subject. Repetition does not guarantee learning, of course, but learning a difficult subject will almost always require some repetition.

Discipling children is a task far more difficult than the toughest advanced placement course in school. Why, then, do we suppose that it is enough to acknowledge the role of parents or to equip them only a few times each year? Responding rightly to such a profound responsibility will require repetition. That is, at least in part, why Moses repeated his plea "lest you forget" seven times in the presence of his people. And that is why, in a family-equipping ministry, constant acknowledgment of parents as primary disciple-makers is a nonnegotiable necessity. Unless this essential implication of God's story line is repeated, we will tend to forget.

IN PRAISE OF INEFFICIENCY

I saw something beautiful yesterday while walking the dog down Breckenridge Lane. In a front yard not far from my home, a young mother was removing leaves from a flower bed—an ordinary activity in the middle of an ordinary day. What was extraordinary about this scene was what I saw beside her. A tow-haired boy, perhaps three or four years old, was attempting to assist her. His rake was adult-sized, his movements were far from efficient, and he was leaving more leaves than he moved. And yet, as I passed this mother and child, I heard no criticisms of his inefficiency. Instead, I heard encouragement and equipping: "Daddy will be so proud of your hard work! Can you try to get those leaves over there?" she asked as she gestured toward a hard-to-reach corner. "You know, honey, it might work better if you turned the rake over."

If this young woman's sole goal for yesterday afternoon was leaf removal, her best bet would have been to plop her preschooler in front of a television to watch professionally produced children's programs that pretend to equip children with skills for life. Then she could have pursued the goal of beautifying the flower bed far more efficiently.

This woman had a goal that was far bigger than any flower bed, though. She understood that her real purpose on this day was not to improve a yard but to shape a soul. She was teaching her child the value of work and partnership and family structures in addition to which side of a rake is supposed to be turned toward the ground. She was an amateur, with no college-transcripted credentials in motherhood or leaf removal. But that was all for the best anyway because no professional program can develop in a child what this mother was engraving in her son's soul yesterday afternoon.

At some point in your transition toward family ministry, you are likely to wonder, "Why do I need to acknowledge parents so frequently as primary faith trainers in their children's lives? No matter how many times I acknowledge them, some parents aren't even trying! Even the ones that are trying don't always do a good job. Wouldn't it be more efficient to expect trained professionals and church programs to do this instead of parents? At the very least, why not simply focus on the parents who get it? Why constantly acknowledge the parents as primary faith trainers when so many parents don't seem to be listening?"

If your sole goal is organizational efficiency, constantly acknowledging the role of parents is probably an inefficient use of your time, and turning over children's spiritual lives to professionals at church would make perfect sense. But efficiency is not the goal of gospel-centered ministry. The crucified and risen Lord Jesus determines the shape and establishes the goal for his church. And it has been his Father's good pleasure to form the church as a conglomeration of amateurs, not as a corporation run by professionals (1 Cor. 12:4–31). The Spirit does not give gifts for the purpose of making the church efficient; he arranges the gifts in the body according to his will to make us holy (1 Cor. 12:11).

The role of God-called leaders in the church is to encourage, acknowledge, and equip fellow members of the church (Eph. 4:11–13) to serve as ministers and missionaries first within their own households, and then far beyond their households (Acts 2:39). These processes are not likely to be quick or efficient. Sometimes, it may feel as if professionalized programs would be an easier solution, but no church program can develop in a child what parents are able to engrave in their children's souls day by day. And so, despite the apparent inefficiency of constantly acknowledging parents as primary faith trainers, family-equipping ministries persist in their passion for telling and training fathers and mothers to disciple their children.

FAMILY-EQUIPPING TRANSITION 4: SYNCHRONIZE

(with W. Ryan Steenburg)

Suppose you implement everything that you've read thus far in this book. Ministry leaders are discipling their families, and their processes of discipleship flow out of a gospel-centered identity. Your ministry is effectively equipping parents for formal faith talks, informal faith walks, and comprehensive faith processes. Suppose that ministries throughout your congregation have worked together to acknowledge parents at every level as primary disciple-makers in their children's lives. In fact, what if it's virtually impossible to attend your church for more than a couple of weeks before hearing how discipling children is one implication of God's transforming work in your heart? What's more, your ministry isn't concerned only with those that are near; families in faith are engaging in as many of these practices as possible with spiritual orphans.

What comes next?

Especially if you are serving in an established church, it's possible that several years will pass before all of these practices are firmly in place. But it can happen. And in many churches and ministries it is happening right now.

But what then? What happens next? How can you pull together these practices into a single, comprehensive approach to ministry?

It's here that the three different models of family ministry diverge most radically. At this point, the family-based model may add intergenerational activities to what's already happening, as well as inviting parents to be involved as much as possible in the discipleship of their children. Family integrated churches eliminate age-organized ministries altogether, replacing them with generationally integrated activities. There are times and contexts where either one of these approaches could be the best approach to family ministry.

The family-equipping ministry model takes a different approach; the last shift is to synchronize and streamline activities that are already in place. Put another way, family-equipping makes certain that every aspect of ministry with children or youth trains, involves, or equips parents as primary disciple-makers in their children's lives.[1] It's what is called the TIE test: If any projected or presently practiced activity for children or youth doesn't clearly train, involve, or equip parents, that activity is either shelved or reworked. Once TIE testing is underway, instead of adding more activities to what you're already doing, you will likely end up restructuring, merging, and even cutting a significant number of activities.

Here's the assumption behind the TIE test: Parents are the people primarily responsible for their children's spiritual development; therefore, what church ministries do with children must never diminish, replace, or bypass what parents are doing. In a family-equipping church, youth and children's ministries exist solely to partner with Christian parents and to supply families in faith for children whose parents are not yet believers. That's why, over time, every aspect of youth and children's ministry must be reoriented to fulfill a different purpose than ever before. Whenever an age-organized activity occurs, the event must operate in clear partnership with believing parents and must guide participants toward a deeper connection with the larger community of believers—and it all begins with the TIE test.

In the space below, develop a strategic question for your ministry. The purpose of the strategic question is to filter activities that might work against equipping parents to disciple their children. For example, the ministry team might ask regarding every activity, "How will this event equip parents to view themselves as primary disciple-makers in their children's lives?" or "How will we train, involve, or equip parents through this activity?" In a full-fledged family-equipping ministry, activities that do not clearly partner with parents as primary disciple-makers are reworked or shelved.
Strategic question:

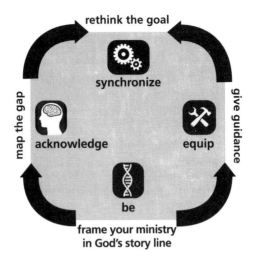

TIE IT ALL TOGETHER

Don't tell him, but we are both a little jealous of our friend Bryan. Whenever Bryan wears a necktie, he has that perfect Windsor knot, complete with the dimple in the middle. Bryan was a successful Boy Scout (he even starred in a Boy Scout commercial in his childhood) so perhaps that's why his neck always seems to be so perfectly knotted. Neither of us has managed to master the fine art of the perfectly dimpled necktie.

Looking at churches that have effectively implemented family-equipping ministry may make you feel like we do when we look at that Windsor knot beneath Bryan's chin. You may feel as if, no matter how many angles you try, family-equipping (or tying the perfect knot) is simply not going to work for you.

When it comes to your church ministries, however, we can offer some significant encouragements, based on what we've observed in churches that have made the transition: Work patiently, carefully, and prayerfully through each ministry and look for creative ways to turn activities that once bypassed parents into vehicles for fulfilling one of three functions: (1) training, (2) involving, or (3) equipping moms and dads.

TRAIN: TURN AGE-SEGMENTED ACTIVITIES INTO TRAINING OPPORTUNITIES FOR PARENTS

The youth head to camp for five days. When they return, they're sleep-deprived, hyper-caffeinated, and ready to change the world. But beyond the babbling summary that mom or dad receives on the car ride home, parents have little idea what triggered such enthusiasm during the week. What information they do receive will be filtered through the sentimental video montage that the youth minister is already rushing to pull together before Sunday morning. Within a week or two, with few exceptions, the fires will have faded in most of the youth, and their habits of life—whether good or bad—will differ little from what was happening before their camp experience.

It isn't only camps that unfold in this way in a significant number of churches, though. It's the weekend spiritual retreats, the student leadership conferences, and the yearly mission trips too. Yet, if parents are primary disciple-makers in their children's lives, shouldn't they also be partners in the spiritual formation that happens through these events? And I don't mean partnership merely in the sense of writing a check, driving a bus, or providing some snacks! Parents must aim at becoming active partners in every aspect of their children's spiritual development—including every age-organized activity that happens through the church.

But how can this work in real life, when events like camps and retreats have been planned for so long without even the slightest reference to the role of parents?

One possibility is to train parents during events so that they can reinforce at home what their children or youth learn at these events. That's what Steve in North Carolina did during a Metamorphosis weekend event for youth. He announced the training for parents and set out fifty chairs, thinking he might be overestimating how many moms and dads would make the effort to be there. When more than two hundred parents showed up, Steve discovered that far more parents desired training than he had guessed at first. I can't guarantee how many parents will show up at your training, but I can guarantee that parents need the training.

Please understand, though: Training of this sort is not a separate and parallel event for parents; that would mean adding a new set of activities instead of redeveloping what you're already doing. It's also not an informational meeting; such orientations are important and necessary at times but they aren't the same as parent training. The point of an informational meeting is to provide, well, information. But you want to do far more in training than merely provide information. The training that we're describing here is a time of equipping parents—typically before or during an event for their children—to apply at home the spiritual truths that their children are learning through the event.

Such training is not an add-on; it's every bit as important as the event itself. So, begin planning the parent training at the same time as, or perhaps even prior to, your planning for the event itself. Conduct the training at a time when as many parents as possible are likely to be present. In some congregations this could mean setting aside Wednesday evening Bible study as a parent training time during the week of youth camp. In another context, it could mean developing a training session immediately after the initial informational meeting for a mission trip.

Regardless of when your church chooses to train parents, coordinate the training carefully with the youth or children's event. The point isn't simply to train parents but to train them to take home what their children are getting at the activity or event. Aim the training toward a single, very specific goal. For example, a training during youth camp might prepare parents and provide resources to lead four weeks of faith talks—one each week—during the month that follows camp. You might even facilitate role-playing during the session so that parents who have never led a faith talk have an opportunity to practice. Or maybe, in a training session that happens during a spiritual retreat, you could work through specific faith walk activities to apply the retreat curriculum in the context of each family's daily life during the following week. You might, for example, provide parents with a list of open-ended questions to prompt discussions with their child throughout the upcoming week. If at all possible, make your training intergenerational; equip older adults to facilitate these training sessions, treating them as honored fathers and mothers in the family of faith (1 Tim. 5:1–2; Titus 2:1–3).

INVOLVE: MOVE BEYOND MERELY INVITING

Without thinking too hard, you could probably tell me exactly who they are. In many smaller and midsized ministries, you wouldn't even need two hands to tally them. What we're talking about are the parents who will actually be present at a typical youth or children's event. What about all the other parents? Well, like you, we tried to let them know that they were welcome to come to the event. But the moment their children exited the minivan and the doors latched, their vehicles careened out of the parking lot and didn't return until the event was over.

If that's what you've experienced in your ministry, we understand why you may be a bit skeptical about our next suggestion, but stay with us for just a moment. Another possibility for synchronizing a ministry event with the lives of families is to involve parents in the event.

Notice that we did not say simply to invite parents to the event—that's what many of us have tried many times before with minimal success. What we are talking about here is *involving* parents in the event. When we merely invite parents to an event, what we're letting parents know is that we want them to be present to support what we've planned, and there are times when such invitations may need to happen. Involving parents is very different from inviting them, though. When we involve parents, we design the experience so that the presence of the parents is necessary for the event to work. Involving parents is likely to require some training. Otherwise, some may try to parent everyone in the youth or children's ministry, while others may focus so strongly on their own children that their involvement isn't helpful to anyone else. Communicate clearly to the parents beforehand what they need to do to make their involvement effective. Be prepared to debrief all parents after the event. If some parents' interactions weren't particularly helpful, pull them aside later and speak to them with gentleness and grace. Regardless of their inadequacies, these parents have still been divinely designated as primary disciple-makers in their children's lives.

And what sorts of events might function well with this degree of parental involvement?

Maybe a youth mission trip where parents lead as crew chiefs and where, each morning, they gather to learn how to lead a family faith talk over a particular biblical text. Then they lead that faith talk with their family members that evening. That way, parents are involved and trained to disciple their families.

What about redesigning preschool ministry for a purpose larger than providing free babysitting during worship celebrations? What if the purpose of the church's nursery became the training of every child to participate in whole church worship celebrations by the time the child turns six? And what if parents became involved in this process once per month, sitting with their child during a miniature worship service? After all, parents are the people who will be overseeing their child in "big church." Why not give parents the opportunity to practice before that time?

What about reworking your small groups for youth and children so that a parent leads an opening devotional each week?

What about morphing the previous generation's weekend youth retreats to become legacy milestone events where parents and families in faith celebrate rites of passage with teenagers?

And what about those children whose parents aren't yet believers in Jesus? That's why having families in faith is so important in a family-equipping faith community! Whenever an event requires the involvement of parents, families in faith joyfully embrace the task of serving as moms and dads for children whose families are not present.

EQUIP: PREPARE PARENTS WITH RESOURCES FOR COSMIC COMBAT

During basic combat training in the United States Army, you are equipped with every resource that you need to be prepared for battle. During nine and a half weeks of training, you receive everything from a triad of physical training outfits to seven pairs of underwear, from four uniforms and two pairs of boots to a fancy pair of eyeglasses affectionately known as BCGs. You receive three meals a day, a ride to any location that isn't within walking distance, and a drill sergeant who's kind enough to always tell you where to go. If it's discovered that soldiers haven't been equipped with a needed resource, American citizens are typically outraged, because it's recognized that soldiers should be prepared to stand against deadly enemies in mortal combat.

As followers of Jesus Christ, our enemy is far more deadly than any foe that a human army might face (1 Pet. 5:8), and, especially when it comes to discipling our families, the stakes are far higher. Parenting and discipling children is cosmic combat against "spiritual forces of evil in the heavenly realms" (Eph. 6:12). Yet, in some churches, the complete corpus of parenting resources consists of a half-dozen faded paperbacks that were published during the Reagan administration, coexisting on a shelf with Bible studies and a few fictive guides how not to be left behind when Jesus returns.

If church members begin surfing the Internet in search of a resource to guide their children's growth, they'll find more than seventy-five thousand books on parenting presently on the market! Faced with such an overwhelming array of resources, some parents will give up. Others will grab whatever book makes the boldest claims about how it can change a child's behavior in the briefest span of time. In most cases, these books will reinforce the parents' tendency to see their children only in light of creation and fall. Parents need guidance and resources to equip them for gospel-centered combat for their children's souls. Yet, in most cases, their churches are not equipping them with such resources.

EQUIPPING THROUGH RESOURCE GUIDES

So how can your ministry equip parents with the resources they need? In the first place, help parents to see that if they are believers in Jesus Christ, God has already equipped them with his Spirit, his Word, and the community of faith (John 16:12–14; Eph. 4:11–16; 2 Tim. 3:16–17; Heb. 13:20–21). Through these gifts from God, it is possible for the gospel to reshape every part of life, including practices of parenting. In whatever problem parents may face, the gospel is foundational to the answer. If it isn't, either we don't understand the problem, or we don't understand the full implications of the gospel.

At the same time, the wisdom of God's people is sometimes expressed through written or recorded resources that point us toward the gospel in every part of life. The point of providing parents with such resources is not to supplement the gospel; the gospel needs no supplement (Gal. 1:6–12).

The point of these resources is to draw from God's work and wisdom in the lives of others to apply the gospel in the lives of parents and children.

With that purpose in mind, develop a brief list of gospel-rich resources that will be helpful to parents in your church. Organize the list by categories with only a couple of books, articles, or podcasts in each category. Too many resources will overwhelm parents. Resources might be organized under headings such as "Tools for Beginning Faith Talks in Your Home," "Celebrating Rites of Passage in Your Home," "How to Have Healthy Conversations with Your Child," "How to Lead Your Child to Christ," "Ideas for Being a Family in Faith for Spiritual Orphans," and so on. Make the resource lists available in the church lobby, tuck them into resource packets for Sunday school teachers, post them on the bulletin board, blog about them on the church website, or develop a men's or women's reading group that reads and reviews the books for the church newsletter. Update the lists at least yearly.

EQUIPPING THROUGH RESOURCE ACTIVITIES

It may be that some youth or children's events can't be shifted to train or involve parents directly. If that's the case, use those events as opportunities to equip parents with resources that recognize their households as primary contexts for discipling their children. For example, if you're the youth minister, you might provide parents with a monthly resource list and some faith walk suggestions that connect with what you're teaching each week in youth group. A children's director might develop a quarterly list of catechism questions and a recommended book that coordinates with the themes that children are exploring in Sunday school. In every instance, your goal is to equip parents with a resource that helps them to rehearse at home the truths that children or youth are learning at church.

Real-Life Ideas for Moving from Segmentation to Synchronization

The point of these ideas is not to provide a step-by-step guide to making the shift from segmentation to synchronization. The point is to spark your thinking by providing you with examples of real-life practices that other ministries have used effectively.

What did the activity look like before?	How did the church choose to change the activity: train, involve, or equip?	What did the activity look like afterward?
Youth attended yearly camp; camp experiences were celebrated in an afterglow service the following Sunday evening.	Train and Equip	Before camp, church staff developed four family faith talk guides that applied what youth would learn at camp. The faith talk guides coordinated visually and thematically with the camp. At the pre-camp parent meeting, parents and families in faith were introduced to these themes and encouraged to pray in specific ways for their youth. Parents and families in faith were also asked to attend a dinner and learning session on Wednesday evening during camp. Using the four faith talk guides, parents and families in faith were trained through this learning experience to engage in four weeks of faith talks with their teenagers. The afterglow service was shifted to serve also as a time of commitment for families and families in faith, to reinforce these themes and teachings through their households.
At the end of the school year, the children's ministry hosted a recreational time to kick off summer programs.	Train and Involve	During the first part of the recreational time, parents and families in faith attended seminars; the themes of these seminars ranged from dressing children modestly to monitoring Internet usage, from how to begin family faith talks to cooking projects to share as a family. After the seminars, the children's recreational time concluded with a competition filled with silly games that didn't depend on skill or numbers, that placed children on teams with their parents or with their families in faith.
Each summer, the church conducted separate youth and adult mission trips.	Involve and Train	One mission trip became a trip that encouraged every father to participate. Fathers served as crew chiefs and, each morning, received training in how to lead a specific family faith talk. Each evening, fathers led their families in that faith talk. Less guidance was given each day to encourage fathers to begin developing faith talks on their own.

The other mission trip became a joint one that brought together the senior adult ministry and the youth ministry. Two seniors—a senior in high school and a senior citizen—partnered together to lead each work crew on the mission trip. *continued* |

Real-Life Ideas for Moving from Segmentation to Synchronization
continued

What did the activity look like before?	How did the church choose to change the activity: train, involve, or equip?	What did the activity look like afterward?
Each year, sixth graders were welcomed into youth group at a special weekend youth retreat.	Involve and Train	The youth retreat became a rite of passage event; prior to the retreat, parents and families in faith were trained to engage with their youth in a series of studies to prepare for adolescence. The retreat culminated with parents and families in faith coming to the campground and participating in a celebration and commissioning that recognized the privileges and responsibilities of the child's growth toward adulthood.
The themes of Sunday morning sermons were never intentionally rehearsed or reinforced at home.	Equip	Each Sunday, a brief faith talk outline began to be provided in the worship folder. The faith talk guide was designed to apply the pastor's message at home. Before the benediction each week, one of the pastors briefly summarized how the faith talk guide might be used at home. The weekly message in youth group was also coordinated to share a text or theme with the weekly faith talk guide and with the pastor's Sunday morning message. The youth minister provided every parent with a brief outline of each week's message with a series of faith walk questions.
During Vacation Bible School, parents dropped off their children each evening. On Friday evening, parents stayed to watch their children perform in a program.	Equip	Beforehand, the church obtained special coupons from several local restaurants and purchased gift cards at three of these restaurants. Additionally, a staff member developed a one-page parents' discussion guide for couples as well as a similar guide for single parents. The discussion guides worked through issues related to children's spiritual development in ways that also presented the gospel. *continued*

Real-Life Ideas for Moving from Segmentation to Synchronization
continued

What did the activity look like before?	How did the church choose to change the activity: train, involve, or equip?	What did the activity look like afterward?
		On Monday evening, parents were required to stay for a brief orientation to the week's events and to sign medical release forms. Parents were informed that they were invited to stay for a second half, to learn how to help their children to develop spiritually. During this second half, in addition to a brief discussion of the role of parents as primary faith trainers, parents were provided with the discussion guides, as well as the restaurant coupons, and encouraged to set aside one evening while their children were at VBS to go out to eat and work through the discussion guide with a spouse (if married), friend, or mentor from church. At the end, three medical release forms were randomly drawn; the parents of those children received the gift cards. Parents were invited to a reception on Friday evening, while their children were preparing for the program, where they were given opportunities to talk about what they learned on their date night as they worked through the discussion guides.

> The gospel is to be rehearsed in the home and reinforced through the church so that Jesus Christ can be revealed with integrity to the world.

Do *not* hand these printed resources to youth or children with the hope that the resources will miraculously make it to mom and dad. I, too, was a captive of this quixotic hope for many years. Then, I became a parent and discovered that such resources rarely survive the trip home. Placed in the hands of children, most resources end up crumpled and laid to rest beneath the car seat amid happy meal toys, secondhand suckers, and stray pieces of cereal. There they remain for months or years, until a parent finally cleans under the seat, a time when family discipleship isn't at the forefront of anyone's mind.

Providing children with papers to clutter the car is not the same as equipping parents with the resources they need to engage in cosmic combat. Handouts for children falls more in the category of killing trees for

Jesus. Whether through a well-produced handout or a well-promoted web page, get the resource directly to the parents. Each time you make contact with the parent, include words of encouragement that recognize the parent's God-given role as a primary disciple-maker in a child's life.

HOW FAMILY-EQUIPPING DOESN'T WORK

If family-equipping happened to be merely about changing an organization, I could stop at this point and say, "Congratulations! Once you've made certain that every activity for youth or children trains, involves, and equips parents, you have completed all the levels. Pat yourself on the back and move on to some other program."

But family-equipping doesn't work that way.

Family-equipping is not a series of steps to success. It is not a programmatic cure-all for your church's problems. It is a process that works its way over time into every aspect of your ministry. And so, synchronizing your ministry is not the ending—far from it! It is the beginning of a bigger and better story for your ministry. This story is bigger because it calls parents to see their children in light of God's great story line of creation, fall, redemption, and consummation. It is better because the goal is not simply healthier families for the church, bigger events for the community, or better ethics for the world. The goal is Jesus, the center is the gospel, and the family is a means for revealing the gospel now and for passing the gospel from one generation to the next.

You may not see the fruit of your family ministry in your lifetime—and that's okay. When it comes to family ministry, multi-generational faithfulness matters far more than momentary success. God has called you to become a minister to generations yet unborn, an equipper who makes disciples with the future in mind.

> **Family-Equipping Ministry in 3D**
>
> *Define* parents as primary disciple-makers.
> *Develop* parents by training, involving, and equipping them for faith talks and faith walks.
> *Direct* parents by providing a clear vision for their children's spiritual development.
>
> (Courtesy of David Wilkinson, strategic plan for CrossRoad Church.)

It helps, now and then, to step back and take a long view. . . .
We accomplish in our lifetime only a tiny fraction
of the magnificent enterprise that is God's work.
Nothing we do is complete. . . .
No statement says all that could be said. . . .
No program accomplishes the church's mission.
No set of goals and objectives includes everything.

This is what we are about:
We plant the seeds that one day will grow.
We water seeds already planted,
knowing that they hold future promise.

We lay foundations that will need further development.
We provide yeast that produces far beyond our capabilities.

We cannot do everything, and there is a sense of liberation
in realizing that. This enables us to do something,
and to do it very well. It may be incomplete,
but it is a beginning, a step along the way,
an opportunity for the Lord's grace to enter and do the rest.

We may never see the end results, but that is the difference
between the master builder and the worker.

We are workers, not master builders; ministers, not messiahs.
We are prophets of a future not our own. Amen.

Adapted from a prayer by Kenneth Untener

FOUNDATION 5
TRANSITION TO
FAMILY-EQUIPPING
FIELD GUIDE

WHAT TO LOOK FOR IN THE FIELD

Gospel-centered synchronization

THE KEY CONSIDERATION

How can the ministry move toward synchronizing every event and activity with what parents and families in faith are doing to disciple children?

HOW TO FIND WHAT YOU'RE LOOKING FOR

Worksheet E: TIE Your Ministry Together

WHAT TO DO

Gather your family ministry team. Finalize a mission statement for your ministry with families. Decide on a unifying strategic question that you will begin to ask about every event or activity for children or youth—a question such as, "How will this event equip parents to view themselves as primary disciple-makers in their children's lives?" or "How will we train, involve, or equip parents through this activity?" Using Worksheet E: TIE Your Ministry Together, list every activity and event in your ministry. Apply the TIE test to each one. Develop ways to train, involve, or equip parents through every activity or event. Make a multiyear plan for reworking each area of ministry, paying special attention to areas where church members or church leaders may be resistant to change.

HOW LONG IT WILL TAKE

Do not attempt to tie your ministry activities to the primary role of parents until your ministry leaders see the discipleship of their families as a response to God's work in their lives ("be"). Begin applying the TIE test when parents cannot avoid hearing about their primary responsibility for their children's spiritual development ("acknowledge") and when the congregation is providing training for parents and families in faith ("equip"). In most congregations, it seems to take three years or so for these processes to take root and another three to five years for them to be fully implemented.

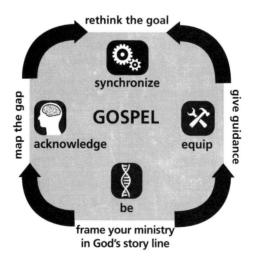

THINK ABOUT IT TOGETHER

Work through these activities with the family ministry team to develop a shared vision for your congregation's family ministry.

1. Develop an in-depth study of 1 Corinthians 12:12—13:13. Consider carefully how coordination of different members in the body of Christ connects with the need to synchronize discipleship in the church with the Christian household.

2. Talk about what it means for family ministry to flow out of a gospel-centered identity. Openly and honestly discuss whether team members are engaged in habits of discipleship in their own households. Offer encouragement and help to one another (Gal. 6:1–5).

3. Pray for your children and grandchildren even if you don't have children or grandchildren yet. Think not simply about managing your children's present behaviors but about whether generations yet to come will know and treasure the gospel. Pray also for the children for whom you will become a family in faith and for their future children.

4. Prayerfully consider what sort of family ministry God has called your congregation to implement. Your family ministry may fit neatly into one of the three categories described in this book (family-equipping, family-based, family-integrated). More likely, your church's family ministry will be a mixture of a couple of different models. Begin a process of rewriting job descriptions in your ministry to reflect what you have learned in this book.

5. Sketch out a multiyear plan to move your ministry toward your chosen ministry model. To turn this plan into a comprehensive strategy for transformation, you may consider working through Aubrey Malphurs, *Advanced Strategic Planning: A New Model for Church and Ministry Leaders* (Grand Rapids, Mich.: Baker, 2005).

RESOURCES TO HELP YOU TRANSITION TO FAMILY-EQUIPPING

Chester, Tim and Steve Timmis. *Total Church: A Radical Reshaping Around Gospel and Community.* Wheaton, Ill.: Crossway Books, 2008.

Haynes, Brian. *Shift: What It Takes to Finally Reach Families Today.* Loveland, Colo.: Group Publishing, 2009.

Hellerman, Joseph. *When the Church Was a Family.* Nashville, Tenn.: B&H Academic, 2009.

Moore, Russell. *Adopted for Life.* Wheaton, Ill.: Crossway Books, 2009.

Younts, John. *Everyday Talk: Talking Freely and Naturally about God with Your Children.* Wapwallopen, Penn.: Shepherd Press, 2005.

AFTERWORD

When I was a kid, my parents read from the big family Bible for devotions. At times, we had to read Scripture verse memory cards at the table before we ate our meal. When we couldn't make it to church on Sunday because of the snow, we had our own church service at home. *Family discipleship* may not have been a common term at the time, but the concept was definitely practiced.

Sometimes I resisted my parents' efforts at family discipleship. But now, those memories are meaningful to me. Looking back, I realize and appreciate the intention and effort it required for my parents to bring up my brothers and me in the nurture and admonition of the Lord (Eph. 6:4).

Upon graduating from a Christian high school, a Christian liberal arts university, and then a theological seminary, I entered into full-time vocational ministry as a youth pastor, desiring to serve God by reaching students with the gospel of Jesus Christ and helping students along their journey as they matured in their faith in Christ. Having been involved with students and youth ministry since 1996, I have learned much about students, parents, children's ministry, youth ministry, and the church as a whole. During these years, it has become clear to me that families who do not take seriously the primary responsibility of discipling their children and students—and children and youth ministries that try to assume this responsibility of discipling children and students—are working against

God's design. As a professor of youth ministry, and one who still advocates the need for youth ministry in the local church, I want to make clear that these issues are not isolated to one side of the equation. The church needs to shoulder the responsibility of training and equipping the parents, and parents need to shoulder the responsibility of being the primary disciplers of their children and students. For those students who do not have parents who are Christ-followers, children's and youth ministries can help fill a gap.

There is a desperate need for churches to take a strong look at how we minister to students and their families. In this book, Dr. Jones has clarified the questions that churches and families need to be asking. Then he says we need to check our motives at the door in order to address this major issue in our culture today. Dr. Jones has given some very practical ways for us to consider and implement family ministry into our mindsets and into the philosophy of ministry by which we organize ourselves and carry out the functions of the church. So as believers, lay leaders, parents, and church leaders, let's take seriously this charge to lead our families and churches in the most biblical ways possible, following God's design for our lives and ministries.

Jonathan Geukgeuzian
Assistant Professor of Youth Ministry
Liberty University Center for Youth Ministries

TWELVE TOOLS TO EQUIP FAMILIES

FOR PARENTS

Bogear, Jim and Jerolyn. *Faith Legacy: Six Values to Shape Your Child's Journey.* Indianapolis, Ind.: Wesleyan Publishing House, 2009.

Farley, William. *Gospel-Powered Parenting: How the Gospel Shapes and Transforms Parenting.* Phillipsburg, N.J.: P&R Publishing, 2009.

Machowski, Marty. *Long Story Short: Ten-Minute Devotionals to Draw Your Family to God.* Greensboro, N.C.: New Growth Press, 2010.

Nappa, Mike and Amy. *Creative Family Prayer Times.* Colorado Springs, Colo.: NavPress, 2007.

Rienow, Rob. *Visionary Parenting: Capture a God-Sized Vision for Your Family.* Nashville, Tenn.: Randall House, 2009.

Trujillo, Kelli B. *Faith-Filled Moments: Helping Kids See God in Everyday Life.* Indianapolis, Ind.: Wesleyan Publishing House, 2009.

FOR MINISTRY LEADERS AND VOLUNTEERS

Chester, Tim and Steve Timmis. *Total Church: A Radical Reshaping Around Gospel and Community.* Wheaton, Ill.: Crossway Books, 2008.

Haynes, Brian. *Shift: What It Takes to Finally Reach Families Today.* Loveland, Colo.: Group Publishing, 2009.

Hellerman, Joseph. *When the Church Was a Family: Recapturing Jesus' Vision for Authentic Christian Community.* Nashville, Tenn.: B&H Academic, 2009.

Moore, Russell. *Adopted for Life: The Priority of Adoption for Christian Families & Churches.* Wheaton, Ill.: Crossway Books, 2009.

Younts, John. *Everyday Talk: Talking Freely and Naturally about God with Your Children.* Wapwallopen, Penn.: Shepherd Press, 2005.

WORKSHEET A:
FAMILY DISCIPLESHIP PERCEPTIONS
AND PRACTICES SURVEY

You may download a printable version of this survey from http://www.wesleyan.org/wph/fmfg/survey. The survey may be reproduced and used freely, as long as no changes are made to it and every copy includes this statement: "Copied from Timothy Paul Jones, *Family Ministry Field Guide* (Indianapolis, Ind.: Wesleyan Publishing House, 2011). Used by permission." If adding items using a scale of 1 to 6 when analyzing data from the surveys, reverse the order of the scale—so that it goes from 6 to 1 instead—on items marked "Reverse Scored."

SURVEY INSTRUCTIONS

This survey is intended for parents with children living at home. If your children are too young to participate in an activity that is described, please honestly assess what you anticipate doing when your children become old enough to participate.

For the purposes of this survey, "church leaders" include pastors, elders, ministers, deacons, teachers, or small group leaders.

Part 1: Parental Perceptions

	Strongly disagree	Disagree	Somewhat disagree	Somewhat agree	Agree	Strongly agree
01. I prioritize consistent family devotional or worship times in my family's schedule.						
02. I would like to do regular family devotions or Bible reading in our home, but my family is just too busy for that right now. It will probably be that way for quite a while.						
03. The church is where children ought to receive most of their Bible teaching.						
04. When my child spontaneously asks a biblical or theological question, I really wish that my child would have asked a minister or other church leader instead of me.						
05. I want to do whatever it takes for my child to succeed in certain sports or school activities—even if that means my family is too busy some weeks to eat any meals together.						
06. Parents, and particularly fathers, have a responsibility to engage personally in a discipleship process with each of their children.						
07. Church leaders are the people primarily responsible for discipling my children and teaching them to share the gospel with others. [REVERSE SCORED]						
08. My church has helped me to develop a clear plan for my child's spiritual growth.						

Part 2: Parental Practices

	Never	Once	A couple of times	Three or four times	Five or six times	Seven or more times
09. Other than mealtimes, how many times in the past *week* have I prayed aloud with any of my children?						
10. How many times in the past *week* has my family eaten a meal together with television, music, and other similar media turned off?						
11. How many times in the past *month* have I read or discussed the Bible with any of my children?						
12. How many times in the past *month* have I discussed any biblical or spiritual matters with any of my children while engaging in day-to-day activities?						
13. How many times in the past *two months* has my family engaged in any family devotional or worship time in our home?						
14. How many times in the past *two months* have I talked with my spouse or with a close friend about my children's spiritual development?						
15. How many times in the past *year* have I intentionally participated with one or more of my children in witnessing to a non-Christian or inviting a non-Christian to church?						
16. How often in the past *year* has any church leader made any contact with me to help me to engage actively in my child's spiritual development?						

WORKSHEET B:
MOTIVES MATTER

PART ONE—PROBLEM-CENTERED PLANNING: DEVELOPING GOALS IN THE WRONG DIRECTION

This is *not* the right way to develop or to implement your goals for family ministry! It does, however, show how we really make plans sometimes. Work through this flowchart individually. Compare your results with other members of the family ministry team. What do you see that is similar in your results? What is different? How did this exercise help you to rethink your motives for moving toward family ministry? Work through this flowchart supposing that your goals are *numeric gains* and *retention*.

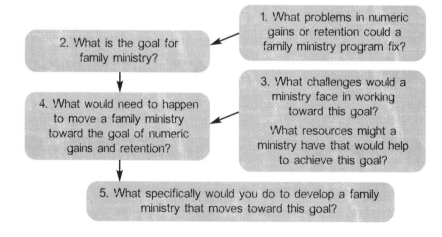

PART TWO—GOSPEL-CENTERED PLANNING: DEVELOPING GOALS BASED ON GOD'S PRIORITIES

This flowchart is a far better example of how to develop plans for our ministries. Work through this flowchart together as a family ministry team.

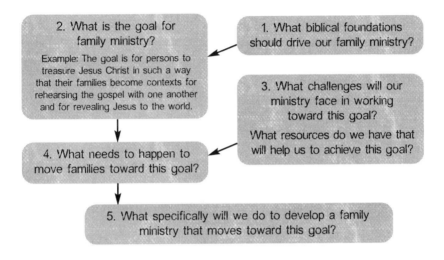

Based on the results from your flowchart, work together to develop a tentative, one-sentence mission statement for your church's ministry to families. Write the statement below.

WORKSHEET C:
LIVING IN GOD'S STORY LINE

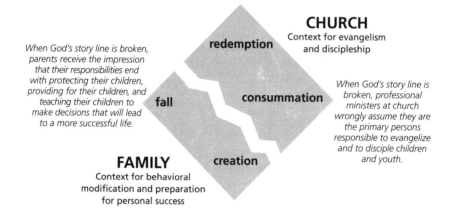

CHURCH
Context for evangelism
and discipleship

When God's story line is broken, parents receive the impression that their responsibilities end with protecting their children, providing for their children, and teaching their children to make decisions that will lead to a more successful life.

redemption

consummation

fall

When God's story line is broken, professional ministers at church wrongly assume they are the primary persons responsible to evangelize and to disciple children and youth.

FAMILY
Context for behavioral modification and preparation for personal success

creation

Look at your church's calendar for the past month.

Place a small X on the redemption/consummation side of the story line above for each activity or event that seeks to evangelize, disciple, or provide fellowship for children or youth.

For each activity or event that intentionally involves and equips parents to function as primary faith trainers in their children's lives, draw a line from the circle for that event to the word *family*.

Imagine that each line is a bridge that connects the generations. Based on this exercise, how many bridges has your congregation built to equip parents to evangelize and disciple their own children?

God has called parents to function as primary faith trainers in their children's lives. Yet, in most cases, churches are not consistently or intentionally connecting parents to the discipleship of their children.

If that's the case in your congregation, what will you do to help parents see their children in light of the whole story line of God?

WORKSHEET D:
WHAT MESSAGE ARE WE SENDING?

On a Sunday morning, take this worksheet and a pen or pencil and walk through the building where your church meets.

Carefully observe the posters, promotional materials, worship folders, and other handouts. Listen carefully to announcements and conversations in several different ministry areas, if possible.

Each time that you read or hear any indication that parents are primary faith trainers in their children's lives, write your observations in the space below.

Based on your observations and the observations of other family ministry team members, how clearly and frequently are parents in your church acknowledged as primary faith trainers in their children's lives?

How thoroughly are parents in your church equipped to engage actively in their children's spiritual development?

In what areas does your church do well when it comes to acknowledging and equipping parents as primary faith trainers in their children's lives?

In what areas can your church do a better job of acknowledging and equipping parents as primary faith trainers in their children's lives?

WORKSHEET E:
TIE YOUR MINISTRY TOGETHER

Look carefully at last year's events and activities in your ministry calendar. As a family ministry team, select ten events or activities to synchronize with faith training at home.

Individually, work through the following process with each event or activity: (1) In the left column, describe the current event or activity. (2) In the center column, choose whether the activity should be shifted to train, involve, or equip parents. (3) In the right column, clearly describe how the activity will be different after synchronization with family faith training. (4) Prioritize the changes; number the events to indicate which ones might be shifted first, then second, and so on.

As a family ministry team, compare the shifts that you have selected and prioritized. Use these suggested shifts to begin to develop a comprehensive plan for moving every aspect of your ministry toward synchronization with faith training at home.

What does the event or activity look like now?	How could your ministry synchronize this event or activity: train, involve, or equip?	What will the event or activity look like afterward?

ACKNOWLEDGEMENTS

This book began with public embarrassment and ended on a day of many tears—all of which sounds much worse than it really was.

I began to sketch out this book after being corrected in a family ministry question-and-answer forum that I moderated. "Practically speaking," I asked the panel, "how can churches become more family centered?" At this point, a pastor (a practitioner who's just as passionate about family ministry as I am) jumped in and said, "I don't want a family-centered church! I want a gospel-centered church that mobilizes families for the glory of God." He apologized afterward for critiquing my choice of words, but there was no need for apology. He was right and it set me to thinking about what family ministry might look like if we started with God's story line instead of beginning with a perceived crisis or with our own vision for healthier families. A few days later, I began writing this book.

As I wrote this book, I was surrounded by colleagues who constantly sharpen me. Hallway conversations with Michael Wilder, Troy Temple, Brian Richardson, and Hal Pettegrew, as well as e-mail correspondence with Jared Kennedy at Sojourn Community Church, shaped and reshaped much of this book. The leaders of The Southern Baptist Theological Seminary and the School of Church Ministries—R. Albert Mohler, Russell Moore, and Randy Stinson, in particular—consistently create an environment where professors can thrive as writers, researchers, and servants of the church.

I am thankful for their support. My Garrett Fellows, doctoral students, and editorial assistants at *The Journal of Family Ministry*—W. Ryan Steenburg, Lilly Park, Derek Brown, and Brian Honett—consistently go above and beyond the call of duty, not only as assistants but also as encouragers, sounding boards, and friends. I could not have written this book without them.

Conversations with Jay Strother at The Church at Station Hill, Brian Haynes at Kingsland Baptist Church, and Steve Wright at Providence Baptist Church contributed to this book in more ways than I can calculate. I am thankful for each of you and for the work that God is doing through you. Mike Nappa of Nappaland Literary Agency continues to make perfect matches between publishers, editors, and my book ideas as well as graciously correcting my tendency to make commitments before thinking about what I'm doing. I completed most of this book on the patio at Starbucks on Frankfort Avenue in Louisville and in the woods at General Butler State Park near Carrollton, Kentucky. I am thankful for the gifts of an Apple iPad and an Amazon Kindle which have untethered me from indoor electrical outlets and weighty bags of books.

Shortly before this book should have been completed, my family changed in a radical way. Seven years ago, my wife and I had adopted Hannah, and I had been quite satisfied with our life as a family of three. But God led us to open our lives to the possibility of caring for "orphans . . . in their affliction" by adopting once again (James 1:27 ESV). And thus began the processes that led our family to adopt a small and quite adorable eight-year-old girl named Skylar. These also happened to be the processes that resulted in this book being far later to the publisher than it ought to have been. I would not trade Skylar for all the promptness in the world, but I am very grateful to Craig Bubeck at Wesleyan Publishing House for his manifold grace and mercy while he awaited the manuscript for this book.

I am finishing this manuscript after a day of many tears—not tears of sadness, mind you, but tears of joy and of good memories.

It has been our last day as a family of three. From tomorrow forward, our family will be a family of four or more. And so today, we celebrated Hannah's past seven years as our only child. We shopped for a new outfit at Target, we had lunch at Incredible Pizza, and we spent a rainy afternoon reading *Star Wars* comic books together at Barnes and Noble—all of Hannah's favorite activities, all celebrated today, all culminated with a God-moment when we shared together our favorite memories from the past seven years. We thanked God, cried, and laughed; and it was good. Tomorrow, our life as a family of four begins, and I will be tweaking some wording in the book over the next few weeks to reflect this unexpected expansion.

Hannah tumbled into our lives as a seven-year-old orphan from Romania, and she has blossomed into a beautiful young woman who is the delight of her daddy's heart. Now, our journey with Hannah continues alongside a new addition. I do not know what the forthcoming years will bring, but I am blessed beyond measure at the possibility of sharing those years with my wife Rayann and our daughters Hannah and Skylar.

Still learning to live as God's child,

Timothy Paul Jones

APPENDIX:
SURVEY METHODOLOGY AND RESULTS

The Family Discipleship Perspectives and Practices Survey: Two hundred seventy-eight parents attending adult Bible study groups in thirty-six different evangelical congregations participated in the survey. Congregations were purposively selected to derive a sample that represented the actual distribution of evangelical church attendees in U.S. American churches in terms of region and church size. Given the approximate total number of parents with children living at home in the United States (35,218,000, U.S. Census Bureau, "America's Families and Living Arrangements: 2010," accessed April 12, 2011, http://www.census.gov/population/www/socdemo/hh-fam/cps2010.html), the percentage of adults in the United States self-identified as connected to evangelical congregations (26.3 percent, http://religions.pewforum.org/affiliations), and the number of persons in the sample, the confidence interval for the results of this study is +/- 5.88 percent with a confidence level of 95 percent. Recommendations in this book may be helpful in nonevangelical and non-U.S. contexts, but the results of the survey should not be generalized to populations outside the United States or to nonevangelical church attendees.

Characteristics and Transitional Patterns in Family-Equipping Churches: The Delphi method study is a widely recognized means for achieving convergence of opinion concerning real-world knowledge solicited from experts on certain topics by means of a group communication process. This study included four iterations (rounds of consultation) with a three-person expert panel that resulted in consensus on eleven items—four related to transitions in organizational ethos and seven related to values and practices. When, as in this particular study that focused on transition to a particular model of family ministry, only a few persons are qualified as experts, smaller samples such as this one have been recognized as acceptable bases for development of consensus by means of Delphi method studies. See S. Lam, et al., "Prediction and Optimization of a Ceramic Casting Process Using a Hierarchical Hybrid System of Neural Networks and Fuzzy Logic," in *IIE Transactions, 32* (2001), 83–92; as well as J.G. Friend, "A Delphi Study to Identify the Essential Tasks and Functions for ADA Coordinators in Public Higher Education," in *Digital Abstracts International, 62* (2001), 1339.

FAMILY DISCIPLESHIP PERCEPTIONS AND PRACTICES SURVEY

Part 1: Parental Perceptions

	Strongly disagree	Disagree	Somewhat disagree	Somewhat agree	Agree	Strongly agree
01. I prioritize consistent family devotional or worship times in my family's schedule.	5 percent	33 percent	17 percent	23 percent	18 percent	5 percent
02. I would like to do regular family devotions or Bible reading in our home, but my family is just too busy for that right now. It will probably be that way for quite a while. [REVERSE SCORED]	8 percent	27 percent	17 percent	32 percent	12 percent	5 percent
03. The church is where children ought to receive most of their Bible teaching. [REVERSE SCORED]	26 percent	45 percent	17 percent	10 percent	2 percent	1 percent
04. When my child spontaneously asks a biblical or theological question, I really wish that my child would have asked a minister or other church leader instead of me. [REVERSE SCORED]	61 percent	31 percent	3 percent	2 percent	2 percent	2 percent
05. I want to do whatever it takes for my child to succeed in certain sports or school activities—even if that means my family is too busy some weeks to eat any meals together. [REVERSE SCORED]	16 percent	27 percent	26 percent	21 percent	10 percent	1 percent

continued

Part 1: Parental Perceptions *continued*

	Strongly disagree	Disagree	Somewhat disagree	Somewhat agree	Agree	Strongly agree
06. Parents, and particularly fathers, have a responsibility to engage personally in a discipleship process with each of their children.	0 percent	0 percent	0 percent	4 percent	34 percent	62 percent
07. Church leaders are the people primarily responsible for discipling my children and teaching them to share the gospel with others. [REVERSE SCORED]	37 percent	44 percent	11 percent	6 percent	0 percent	1 percent
08. My church has helped me to develop a clear plan for my child's spiritual growth.	18 percent	41 percent	17 percent	18 percent	6 percent	1 percent

Part 2: Parental Practices

	Never	Once	A couple of times	Three or four times	Five or six times	Seven or more times
09. Other than mealtimes, how many times in the past *week* have I prayed aloud with any of my children?	21 percent	11 percent	14 percent	13 percent	20 percent	21 percent
10. How many times in the past *week* has my family eaten a meal together with television, music, and other similar media turned off?	5 percent	5 percent	28 percent	31 percent	25 percent	5 percent
11. How many times in the past *month* have I read or discussed the Bible with any of my children?	20 percent	10 percent	25 percent	10 percent	9 percent	26 percent
12. How many times in the past *month* have I discussed any biblical or spiritual matters with any of my children while engaging in day-to-day activities?	7 percent	2 percent	21 percent	19 percent	20 percent	31 percent
13. How many times in the past *two months* has my family engaged in any family devotional or worship time in our home?	35 percent	10 percent	21 percent	6 percent	5 percent	22 percent
14. How many times in the past *two months* have I talked with my spouse or with a close friend about my children's spiritual development?	18 percent	6 percent	26 percent	16 percent	13 percent	20 percent

continued

Part 2: Parental Practices *continued*

	Never	Once	A couple of times	Three or four times	Five or six times	Seven or more times
15. How many times in the past *year* have I intentionally participated with one or more of my children in witnessing to a non-Christian or inviting a non-Christian to church?	44 percent	9 percent	27 percent	14 percent	2 percent	4 percent
16. How often in the past *year* has any church leader made any contact with me to help me to engage actively in my child's spiritual development?	68 percent	12 percent	14 percent	5 percent	0 percent	2 percent

NOTES

CHAPTER 1

1. FamilyLife, *Family Needs Survey: National Database: August 2008* (Little Rock, Ark.: FamilyLife Church and Pastor Relations Office, 2008).

CHAPTER 2

1. Chap Clark, *The Youth Worker's Handbook to Family Ministry: Strategies and Practical Ideas for Reaching Your Students' Families* (Grand Rapids, Mich.: Zondervan, 1997), 13.

2. Jim Burns, "What Is Family-Based Youth Ministry?" accessed December 13, 2010, http://www.youthworker.com/youth-ministry-resources-ideas/youthministry/11624050.

3. Read Selma Wilson, Rodney Wilson, and Scott McConnell, *The Parent Adventure: Preparing Your Children for a Lifetime with God* (Nashville, Tenn.: B&H, 2008) for this study.

CHAPTER 3

1. Mark Oestreicher, *Youth Ministry 3.0: A Manifesto of Where We've Been, Where We Are, and Where We Need to Go* (Grand Rapids, Mich.: Zondervan, 2009), Kindle edition, chap. 1.

2. See Brandon Shields, "Family-Based Ministry: Separated Contexts, Shared Focus" in *Perspectives on Family Ministry: Three Views,* ed. Timothy Paul Jones (Nashville, Tenn.: B&H Academic, 2009), 98–120; and Brandon Shields, "An Assessment of Dropout Rates of Former Youth Group Participants in Conservative Southern Baptist Megachurches" (Ph.D diss., The Southern Baptist Theological Seminary, 2008). The individual with whom the 90 percent attrition rate originated stated in a personal interview with Brandon Shields in September 2006, that he never intended this information to serve as a published statistic.

3. Victor Lee and Jerry Pipes released a book entitled *Family to Family: Leaving a Lasting Legacy* (Alpharetta, Ga.: North American Mission Board, 1999) in which they suggested that 88 percent of evangelical youth drop out of the church after high school graduation. This statistic seems to have been based on their personal recollections from

their own experiences in youth ministry. This statistic was picked up and quoted numerous times; see "SBC Calls for Cultural Engagement; Education Resolution Declined" (June 2004), accessed December 13, 2010, http://www.bpnews.net/BPnews.asp?ID=18501; and, "Family Life Council Says It's Time to Bring Family Back to Life" (June 2002), accessed December 13, 2010, http://www.sbcannualmeeting.net/sbc02/newsroom/newspage.asp?ID=261.

4. In a 2006 study from the Barna Research Group, more than four out of five teens say they had attended a church for a period of at least two months during their teenage years (81 percent). A majority of twenty somethings (61 percent) had been churched at one point during their teen years but then disengaged, no longer actively attending church, reading the Bible, or praying. One-fifth of twentysomethings (20 percent) have maintained a level of spiritual activity consistent with their high school experiences. Another one-fifth of teens (19 percent) were never significantly reached by a Christian community of faith during their teens and have remained disconnected from the Christian faith (George Barna, "Most Twentysomethings Put Christianity on the Shelf Following Spiritually Active Teen Years," accessed December 13, 2010, http://www.barna.org/barna-update/article/16-teensnext-gen/147-most-twentysomethings-put-christianity-on-the-shelf-following-spiritually-active-teen-years). In a 2002 study, George Gallup determined that 51 percent of sixteen- to seventeen-year-olds are involved in a faith community while 32 percent of eighteen- to twenty-nine-year-olds are engaged, suggesting a net attrition rate of 38 percent. Gallup defined faith community involvement as attendance in the past seven days (George H. Gallup, Jr., "The Religiosity Cycle," accessed December 13, 2010, http://www.gallup.com/poll/6124/Religiosity-Cycle.aspx). For the 70 percent figure, see LifeWay, "LifeWay Research Uncovers Reasons 18 to 22 Year Olds Drop Out of Church," accessed December 13, 2010, http://www.lifeway.com/article/165949. Research from an Adventist scholar reported an attrition rate of 49 percent among Adventist young adults with a significant number returning to Adventist congregations when they are married or become parents (Roger Dudley, *Why Our Teenagers Leave the Church* [Hagerstown, Md.: Review and Herald, 1999], 35). However, more recent research has suggested that parenthood does not in fact bring significant numbers of young adults back to church. Only one out of twenty parents said that having children helped them to become active in church for the first time; 17 percent of parents said that having a child encouraged them to reconnect with church after a period of not attending. Four percent of parents said that having children actually decreased their church involvement ("Parenthood Does Not Make for Active Churchgoers," [Barna Research Group], accessed December 27, 2010, http://www.christianpost.com/article/20100524/study-having-kids-does-not-make-parents-active-churchgoers). This pattern of dropouts and returns is apparently not a recent phenomenon. Data from the 1970s suggested that 46 percent of persons disengaged from their faith communities at some point during their lives; 51 percent—perhaps more—of these persons eventually reengaged with church (D. Roozen, "Church Dropouts: Changing Patterns of Disengagement and Re-Entry," *Review of Religious Research Supplement* [1980], 427–450). For the 88 percent retention rate in some megachurches, see Brandon Shields, "An Assessment of Dropout Rates of Former Youth Group Participants in Conservative Southern Baptist Megachurches" (Ph.D diss., The Southern Baptist Theological Seminary, 2008).

5. "Estimated Median Age at First Marriage, by Sex: 1890 to the Present," United States Census Bureau, accessed December 13, 2010, http://www.census.gov/population/socdemo/hh-fam/ms2.pdf.

6. Dietrich Bonhoeffer, *Life Together: The Classic Exploration of Faith in Community* (New York: Harper, 1954), 21.

CHAPTER 5

1. "Britain: Embattled but Unbowed," *Time* (16 February 1981), accessed December 13, 2010, http://www.time.com/time/magazine/article/0,9171,954658,00.html.

2. Paraphrased from Rob Plummer, "Bring Them Up in the Discipline and Instruction of the Lord," in *Trained in the Fear of God: Family Ministry in Theological, Historical, and Practical Perspective,* eds. Randy Stinson and Timothy Paul Jones (Grand Rapids, Mich.: Kregel, 2011).

3. Iohannis Chrysostomi, *Interpretatio Omnium Epistularum Paulinarum,* ed. F. Field (Oxford, U.K.: Clarendon, 1847), 4:323.

4. Augustinus Hipponensis, *De Doctrina Christiana* (n.p., n.d.), 4:28:29. For a contemporary expression of this same theme, see Greg Ogden, *Transforming Discipleship: Making Disciples a Few at a Time* (Downers Grove, Ill.: IVP, 2003), 65.

CHAPTER 7

1. Two other recent research projects have reported similar findings. In a Barna Research Group study, nearly nine out of ten parents with elementary-aged children identified parents as the people primarily responsible for training children in religious beliefs and values. Only 11 percent placed this responsibility on the church ("Parents Accept Responsibility for Their Child's Spiritual Development but Struggle with Effectiveness," Barna Research Group, accessed December 13, 2010, http://www.barna.org/barna-update/article/5-barna-update/120-parents-accept-responsibility-for-their-childs-spiritual-development-but-struggle-with-effectiveness). In a LifeWay Research study, 83 percent of parents identified parents as the persons primarily responsible for their children's spiritual development (Mark Kelly, "LifeWay Research Looks at Role of Faith in Parenting," accessed December 13, 2010, http://www.lifeway.com/article/168935).

CHAPTER 8

1. In a LifeWay Research study, 25 percent of parents defined their purpose in parenting as raising children who would become "happy adults," 25 percent mentioned "good values," while 22 percent stated "finding success in life." Only 9 percent mentioned godliness or having faith in God (Mark Kelly, "LifeWay Research Looks at Role of Faith in Parenting," accessed December 13, 2010, http://www.lifeway.com/article/168935).

2. Richard Ross and Ken Hemphill, *Parenting with Kingdom Purpose* (Nashville, Tenn.: B&H, 2005), 7.

3. Walt Mueller, "Why I Am Rich," Center for Parent/Youth Understanding, accessed December 13, 2010, http://www.todaysyouthculture.com/Page.aspx?id=469426.

4. A recent worldwide study of the presence and effect of people's busy-ness revealed that, for two out of three pastors, busyness gets in the way of their relationship with God. See Michael Zigarelli, "Distracted from God: A Five-Year Worldwide Study," accessed December 13, 2010, http://www.epiphanyresources.com/9to5/articles/distractedfromgod.htm.

5. For 81 percent of parents never having been acknowledged or contacted regarding their children's spiritual development, see "Parents Accept Responsibility for Their Child's Spiritual Development but Struggle with Effectiveness," Barna Research Group, accessed December 13, 2010, http://www.barna.org/barna-update/article/5-

barna-update/120-parents-accept-responsibility-for-their-childs-spiritual-development-but-struggle-with-effectiveness. For youth ministry values expressed through time and budgets, see Daniel Broyles, "An Analysis of S.B.C. Youth Ministry Programmatic Values Investigated through Financial Expenditures and Ministerial Activities" (Ph.D. diss., The Southern Baptist Theological Seminary, 2009).

6. FamilyLife, *Family Needs Survey: National Database: August 2008* (Little Rock, Ark.: FamilyLife Church and Pastor Relations Office, 2008).

CHAPTER 10

1. Chap Clark, "From Fragmentation to Integration: A Theology for Contemporary Youth Ministry, accessed April 11, 2011, http://www.forministry.com/vsItemDisplay.dsp&objectID=E72737BD-864C-4E53-A419FFCE44955BCF&method=display&templateID=C3435351-D45C-4B52-867A3F794D1CD85C.

2. Chap Clark, *The Youth Worker's Handbook to Family Ministry* (Grand Rapids, Mich.: Zondervan, 1997), 24.

3. Synthesized from Herbert Stachowiak, *Allegmeine Modelltheorie* (New York: Springer, 1973), 20–24, 254–264, 320–331; Wilhelm Dangelmaier, *Fertigungsplanung* (New York: Springer, 2001), 11–13; Albert Karer, *Optimale Prozessorganisation im IT-management* (Berlin, Germany: Springer, 2007), 21; Bernd Reinhoffer, *Heimatkunde und Sachunterricht im Anfangsunterricht* (Bad Heilbrunn, Germany: Klinkhardt, 2000), 50.

CHAPTER 11

1. Roland H. Bainton, *Here I Stand: A Life of Martin Luther*, rep. ed. (Peabody, Mass.: Hendrickson, 2009), 307.

CHAPTER 12

1. Christian Smith with Melinda Lundquist Denton, *Soul Searching: The Religious and Spiritual Lives of American Teenagers* (Oxford, U.K.: Oxford University Press, 2005), 56.

2. 1 *Clement* 21:8; Ignatius of Antioch, *To the Philadelphians,* 4:5; *Martyrdom of Justin,* 4.

CHAPTER 13

1. For "God sightings" see Brian Haynes, *Shift: What It Takes to Finally Reach Families Today* (Loveland, Colo.: Group Publishing, 2009). For "hullabaloo" see Timothy Paul Jones, *Hullabaloo: Discovering Glory in Everyday Life* (Colorado Springs: Cook, 2007).

2. Adapted from Legacy Milestones, accessed April 11, 2011, http://www.legacymilestones.com.

3. John Wesley, "On Family Religion," *Sermons on Several Occasions* vol. 2 (New York: Carlton and Phillips, 1855), 300–306.

CHAPTER 15

1. The TIE test is adapted from the "RTI Principle" found in Steve Wright with Chris Graves, *ReThink: Decide for Yourself, Is Student Ministry Working?* (Raleigh, N.C.: InQuest Ministries, 2007).

ABOUT THE AUTHOR

Dr. Timothy Paul Jones is a CBA best-selling and award-winning author, scholar, and professor of discipleship and family ministry at The Southern Baptist Theological Seminary. He has earned the bachelor of arts degree in biblical studies, a master of divinity with concentration in church history and New Testament, as well as the doctor of philosophy degree.

Dr. Jones has authored, coauthored, or contributed to more than a dozen books. He has also contributed numerous articles to popular ministry magazines and academic journals such as *Discipleship Journal; Preaching: The Professional Journal for Pastors; Proclaim: The Journal for Biblical Preaching; Leading Adults; Religious Education Journal; Christian Education Journal; Perspectives in Religious Studies; Bibliotheca Sacra; Midwestern Journal of Theology;* and many others. Dr. Jones has written nearly two hundred entries in two highly-regarded reference works, *Nelson's Dictionary of Christianity* and *Nelson's New Christian Dictionary.* Dr. Jones has been the recipient of the Baker Book House Award in Theological Studies, the North American Professors of Christian Education Scholastic Recognition Award, and the 2009 Retailers' Choice Award from Christian Retailing. While serving as senior pastor of First Baptist Church of Rolling Hills in Tulsa, Oklahoma, he taught biblical languages at Oklahoma Baptist University's Ministry Training Institute and served as adjunct professor of Greek at Midwestern Baptist Theological Seminary.

Despite his strong academic pedigree, Dr. Jones has shown a unique ability to communicate in an appealing, reader-accessible style that has made him popular with the masses through books such as the best-selling *The DaVinci Codebreaker* (coauthored with James Garlow), *Misquoting Truth* (a defense of the trustworthiness of the New Testament texts), and *Christian History Made Easy* (a user-friendly guide to church history). Dr. Jones has been a regular guest on the weekly television talk-show *Moral Side of the News*, the longest-running community service program in North America. He has also been featured on Fox News and WGN, commenting on religious trends and topics.